BEYOND JULES VERNE

Also by Robin Knox-Johnston

A World of My Own
Sailing Last But Not Least
Twilight of Sail
The BOC Challenge 1986
(*with Barry Pickthall*)
The Cape of Good Hope
Seamanship
Columbus Venture
Sea, Ice and Rock
(*with Chris Bonington*)
Cape Horn

Beyond Jules Verne

Circling the world in a record-breaking 74 days

Robin Knox-Johnston

CORONET BOOKS
Hodder and Stoughton

First published in Great Britain in 1995
by Hodder & Stoughton
A division of Hodder Headline PLC

A Coronet paperback 1995

10 9 8 7 6 5 4 3 2 1

A CIP catalogue record for this title is available from
the British Library

ISBN 0 340 64704 3

Printed and bound in Great Britain by
Cox & Wyman Ltd, Reading, Berkshire

Hodder and Stoughton
A division of Hodder Headline PLC
338 Euston Road
London NW1 3BH

To my countryman
Phileas Fogg

CONTENTS

CHARTS

ILLUSTRATIONS

Section 1

Tag about to be lifted into the water
Stepping Enza's carbon fibre mast
Enza emerges after her first refit
Moored astern of Commodore in Brest harbour[1]
A crew cabin in one of the floats[2]
In the galley
The chart table in the godpod
Enza at speed with fully reefed mailsail
Craning out at Cape Town
The damaged dagger board
The hole in the hull
With Bruno at Commodore's triumph
Olivier de Kersuason[3]
The team for the second attempt[4]
An increase in pace after the second refit
Leading Lyonnaise out from Brest[5]

Section 2

Angus and George eat on deck
Jaws short-circuits the washing up
Waiting for a South Atlantic squall
David brings tea to the cockpit

Crossing from hull to godpod in heavy weather
Lowering the mainsail
Getting ready for a sail change
Southern Ocean icebergs
Hat-making in the South Atlantic
Robin wearing the result
An ugly confused sea near the finish
The destroyer's view[6]
Sprinting for the line
The crew celebrates

Photographic credits

1   Mark Pepper/Pickthall Picture Library
2   Peter Bentley/Pickthall Picture Library
3   Pierre Saboulin/Pickthall Picture Library
4   Mike Hewitt/Allsport
5   Pickthall Picture Library
6   Barry Pickthall/Pickthall Picture Library

Front of jacket photograph: Rob Tucker
Back of jacket photograph: Stephen Munday/Allsport
All other photographs belong to the author.

AUTHOR'S NOTE

To the New Zealand apple-growers one can only say thanks for making it all possible and I hope the market expands as a reward. Thanks, too, to Joe Pope and Brian Aitken for picking up the idea so quickly in the first place.

Preparing and undertaking a voyage requires a huge team of people, from the builders, equipment and sailmakers, through the suppliers of stores and finally the crew and their long-suffering families. Others, like Peter Dunning and Val Hatch, put their houses at our disposal in Portsmouth, Rhode Island, where the first BOC Challenge Committee turned out in force to help us get ready. It is true to say that the ultimate success was in no small measure due to Rob Rice's weather predictions but the project could never have happened if the Carbospars team had not achieved a miracle by completing a major refit in just six weeks. They were not alone, Autohelm supplied the electronic pilots, wind and speed instruments, and these, together with Skanti Radio and Raytheon weatherfax were all initially installed by Maricom of Hamble. Messrs Bridport Gundry supplied the netting that bridged the gaps between the hulls, creating a vast, safe working platform. The brilliant paint finish was due to International Paints and sails were supplied by Banks, North and Lidgard. We operated from Hamble Point Marina thanks to Mark Bowden, where Seastart provided us with a first-class towing service in and out of the river. McDougalls were responsible for our 6000-calorie a day diet, and Patak sent me the very large jar of lime pickle the contents of which disappeared so quickly. Whilst we were away our families were kept closely informed of our progress by Theresa Cash of Michael Humphreys and Partners, who were the PR agents in the UK. To my wife Sue for the typing, correcting and reading and Maggie Body of Hodder and Stoughton, my grateful thanks for being so hard working and patient.

Finally we must apologise to all those who found a floating tennis court hurtling towards them at 30 mph in the Solent a shock – we had to work up somewhere!

Facing page: Designer, Nigel Irens' drawing of *Enza*, showing the carbon fibre mast and her final sailplan with the hulls extended to 85 feet. Before the successful attempt 5 feet were added to the stern, 2 feet to the bows, and the underwater hull shape changed.

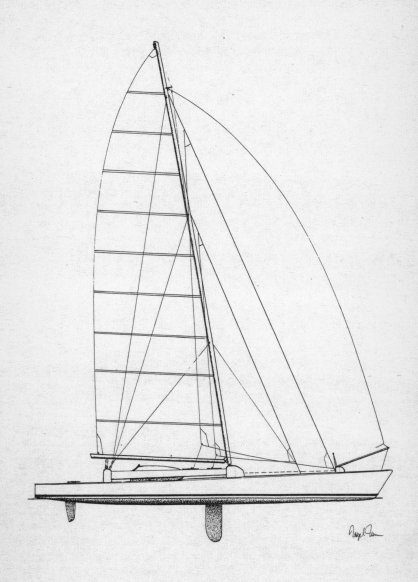

1

Can Jules Verne Be Bettered?

"Are you going to Paris for the Jules Verne announcement?" I asked Peter Blake as we walked across the yard at the Whitbread Brewery in Chiswell Street.

"Thought I might. As long as they give us a date I can attend," he answered, and then added, "I've been working on some plans for a rather unusual boat to try for it."

"Oh, yes?" I responded encouragingly. "My scheme's for a traditional catamaran. What's yours?"

It was the 2nd July 1992 and we had been in the City attending a Whitbread Race committee meeting. What we were discussing now was the forthcoming announcement by the French Minister of Culture of a trophy and a million dollars' prize money for the first boat to sail round the world, without outside assistance, in less than the author Jules Verne's famous eighty days.

The concept, like Jules Verne, was very French and a tribute to their imagination. A small committee, l'Association Jules Verne, had been established to supervise the organisation. Leading it was Florence Arthaud, one of the toughest women sailors around and recent winner of the French single-handed race from St Malo to Guadaloupe, the Route de Rhum. Another member was Titouan Lamazou, also French, who was a natural since he held the current circumnavigation record of 109 days, 8 hours, 48 minutes and 50 seconds, which he had, in fact, achieved single-handed. Peter and I had been invited along to provide an international flavour. The announcement of the trophy was set for the autumn and both Florence and Titouan were planning to go for the record themselves. Indeed, Titouan had an enormous monohull nearing completion for the purpose.

In the wings, but refusing to join the Association, was the controversial French media celebrity and very experienced sailor, Olivier de Kersuason, who was planning to beat eighty days as well with a 90-foot trimaran, *Charal*, in which, under the name *Poulain*, he had already completed a single-handed circumnavigation of 125 days.

"How are you getting on with finding sponsorship?" I asked Peter. It was the inevitable stumbling block.

"No luck so far." He shrugged. "You know what it's like. You've got to win or sink to get any attention these days. But this Jules Verne idea's nice and simple and worth a go. I've not given up yet."

Conventional yacht racing is difficult for the general public to grasp, mainly because of the confusion caused by various highly complicated handicap systems. One exception is a match race like the America's Cup, or a one-design, where all the craft are identical and the first past the post is the winner. But the problem remains that most of the action takes place out of sight of land. The beauty of the Jules Verne challenge was that it would be possible to make a daily comparison of actual progress against the target distance needed to complete a circumnavigation in under eighty days, and this would be quite clear to someone who knew nothing about sailing. You would be either ahead or behind – simple.

I was surprised that Peter had not managed to find sponsorship yet. Since he had won the previous Whitbread Race so convincingly, not just the race overall but every single leg, I would have thought he would have had no difficulty in acquiring backing for a project like this in his native New Zealand. But my luck in the UK had been no better. I gave vent to my frustration.

"It's a crying shame. The French will pull it off first again because they have the imagination and the support. After all, if you can't get the finance in New Zealand and I cannot find it here, then I don't see much opposition to Titouan and Olivier coming from the Anglo-Saxons."

The conversation paused.

"How about teaming up?" said Peter suddenly.

"Why not," I responded without hesitation.

Peter and I have known each other since 1970 when he applied to join Les Williams and me as crew for the first Cape Town – Rio Race in the 71-foot yacht *Ocean Spirit*, in which we had just won the two-handed Round Britain Race (the only occasion that race has been won by a monohull). When we came to organise the watches Peter was one of our watch leaders and we won line honours in Rio. When Les and Alan Smith put together a project for the first Whitbread Race in 1973 Peter was a watch leader again. They got just beyond Cape Town when damage forced them to withdraw, but Peter and Les raced again in the 1974 Round Britain Race in *Burton Cutter*. Les and I entered the 1977 Whitbread, this time with a 77-foot maxi-racer, *Heath's Condor*. We intended to box and cox the race by taking it in turns to skipper the boat, so we needed a good mate to provide continuity for the crew. Peter was our unanimous choice and replied immediately to our telegram. So over the years we had covered a few sea miles together, which is always a good start to a new sailing project, but, more importantly, we seemed to see nautical matters the same way.

Reducing an existing record of 109 days to under eighty is an incredible leap. It is not as if 109 days is slow, it is extremely fast, an average of 250 miles a day or roughly 10.5 knots. In the past the fastest of the great clipper ships, the pinnacle of commercial sail development, had only managed to average 8 knots for a complete circumnavigation. So, although the times were gradually reducing over the years, in order to bring 109 down to eighty days required an enormous improvement of thirty-six per cent, to an average distance of 341 miles per day or a speed of 14.2 knots. This was faster than the capabilities of all but a handful of the yachts afloat in 1992, and then might only be achieved in exceptionally favourable conditions. All of us involved in the Association were convinced that it just might be possible to maintain such a rate for eighty days if we went for very large boats built to the limit of modern techniques, but our solutions varied considerably.

Titouan's idea of the giant monohull yacht might work. The formula for calculating a boat's maximum speed is

$$\sqrt{\text{waterline length}} \times 1.4$$

approximately, the 1.4 changing a bit with hull shapes. So Titouan, theoretically, should have a top speed of 15.5 knots, but the margin between his top speed and the average speed needed was far too close realistically, as he would constantly have to achieve ninety-two per cent of his best speed. In recent years some of the most interesting developments in sailing yachts have come in the Open 60-foot class, where the lack of restrictions, apart from length, have produced some very exciting boats, not least Titouan's previous record-breaker, and his new plan was just scaling up from there. It would be a fascinating challenge, he would almost certainly set a new world record, but we doubted he would beat eighty days.

Olivier in his trimaran was another matter. The speed of a multihull is not governed by the same rule as for monohulls and they will go faster than a monohull of similar length. *Charal* was enormous, the largest racing multihull afloat in the world, and he had done considerable mileage with her. If it came to a straight contest between the 120-foot monohull and the 90-foot trimaran, my money would have to be on the trimaran.

Both Titouan's and Olivier's boats were already in existence and planning to set out in December 1992, whereas all the other contenders were still at the concept stage and unlikely to be on the water by that date. This departure time was chosen to ensure the most dangerous part of the voyage, the passage through the roaring forties of the Southern Ocean, would be during the southern summer. Florence Arthaud was not reckoning on being ready for this competition, she was negotiating the sponsorship for a 120-foot multihull, a real monster, which she was certain would beat eighty days – we did not argue with her!

Peter started to describe to me his ideal boat. She was to be a large lightweight monohull with an impressively big rig. The righting lever to support the sail area at high wind speeds was to be provided, not by the traditional heavy lead keel, but by a pod on each side, the weather one of which could be extended out from the main hull and filled with water whilst the leeward one remained empty. The resulting vessel was not unlike a *proa*, the Polynesian twin-hulled craft in which the mast is on one hull and the crew balance the sail by placing themselves on the other one, except that a huge crew would be required to supply sufficient weight to balance this particular rig, so they were replaced by water. Powerful electric pumps would fill the pod and there would be a very simple dumping mechanism so the water could be discharged in a hurry if the boat was caught aback or needed to tack quickly. In many respects it was a trimaran with a small keel and without the floats, and the concept owed much to Peter's involvement with *Steinlager 1*, a 60-foot trimaran in which he had won the first two-handed Round Australia Race. It was the hammering the outriggers were subjected to in really rough weather, to the extent that one had fallen off when the boat was being delivered back to New Zealand after the race, which encouraged him to look for an alternative solution in the search for high speed. It was a neat idea, but one that would probably need considerable development and that would take time, which we did not have.

My own thoughts had followed what was, for me by now, a traditional line. My first encounter with multihulls was an outing in Brightlingsea on a snowy cold February morning in 1974 in a Tornado with Reg White, then the world champion in the class and subsequently the Olympic gold medallist. My bewilderment started before we set off when we hauled on our wet suits and Reg went over to the tap and filled his boots with hot water. His explanation was simple. As we were bound to fill our boots during the course of the morning anyway, we might as well start with warm water, so the shock when the sea got in would be less! We set off, but within 600 feet Reg beached the boat and ordered me to pick up the front. I stood there for four or five minutes, listening to the slight sound of running water from aft where Reg was fiddling. Then I was told to lower the boat and we could relaunch her. Back afloat I asked Reg what he had been up to.

"Just putting the bungs in," he said. "We'd look a bit silly if we sank the first time we sailed together, wouldn't we?"

It was encouraging to know that even world champions can forget something so obvious!

Reg was building a 70-foot catamaran for us at the time, us being an organisation called British Challengers. The boat, which was to be sailed by Gerry Boxall and myself, was later christened *British Oxygen* and when complete she was the largest racing multihull built to date. She was experimental insofar as no one really knew in 1974 what strains might be expected on a structure so large. The hulls were made from glass-reinforced plastic in a mould and the beams were of aluminium with a special dolphin-striker beneath the main beam to counter the enormous downward pressure from the mast. Perhaps the most interesting features were the dagger boards, made by British Aerospace and operated by hydraulic rams from the cockpit. At that time multihulls were still perceived as extreme and also incapable of sailing close to the wind. *British Oxygen*, with her very effective dagger boards, could point as high as any monohull. In fact we once sailed her through a Solent-based offshore fleet pointing higher and footing faster. We won the 1974 Round Britain Race with her in record time and then she was sold to the French, who lost her in their first race as owners in mid-Atlantic. The power of the craft was immensely impressive and, although heavy compared with modern multihulls, she was a third of the weight of an equal length monohull and the speed on a reach with the wind above force 6 coming from abaft the beam was awesome; 20 knots seemed slow in those conditions.

My next multi, built by Reg again seven years later, used the same moulds as *British Oxygen* but the designer, Rod Macalpine Downie, made basic changes to the sheer. The new catamaran, which was christened *Sea Falcon*, was the same length but less than half the weight. Without her mast and sails she weighed in at only 4.3 tons. By now large multihulls were by no means uncommon, the French had a fleet of them, but *Sea Falcon* was always in the running and had there been a steady sponsor she would have been extremely successful. We lost her in the end when we were run down off Cape Finisterre by a vessel that did not stop, probably unaware of what it had done. The lasting impression of her, apart from 32 knots in Portland Harbour on one occasion, was the way she handled a hurricane off Cape Hatteras. In northerly winds and with a north-setting current the Gulf Stream ensured a very difficult choppy sea, but having run away down one wave and crashed into the back of the wave in front, an action that decelerated us from 25 to nil knots in micro-seconds, we left up a handkerchief of sail and kept the boat slightly down from abeam to the waves. She was not always comfortable. Indeed, on one occasion a wave breaking over the deck is probably what stopped us being tipped over, but we did survive and that gave me enormous confidence in a catamaran's ability to handle heavy weather conditions.

The next craft was again a Macalpine Downie design, but 60 feet and named after her sponsor, *British Airways*. We built her expressly to break the New York to San Francisco record, so she was tough and not particularly light. This time the hulls were cold moulded, using mahogany, and I built her with a small team in an old maltings in Ipswich, a procedure made necessary when the original builders went bankrupt. She showed her breeding as a seaboat as far as I was concerned in the first race we tried her out on, the Ruta del Escrubimento from Spain to Santo Domingo in the Dominican Republic (half the Caribbean island that used to be called Hispaniola which it shares nervously with Haiti). We met a hurricane on the way across and ran before the wind to get out of it. Then the same hurricane returned and caught us again off the north coast of Hispaniola on Christmas Day, rather late in the season. We lay hove-to as it blew past, our only consolation being that the huge liner *Norway*, ex-*France*, was also hove-to only a hundred miles away.

I was immensely encouraged by our survival of these extreme weather conditions and turned to the New York – San Francisco record as the next objective. Personnel at the sponsors had changed however and the new people decreed that Cape Horn might be dangerous. They even asked if I had ever been there! So we were forced to content ourselves with the normal multihull racing circuit in which we could not expect to be competitive, though by dint of always finishing, and winning our class in the Monaco – New York Race, we actually won the Class 2 World Championship in 1986 and set a British transatlantic sailing record which still stands today. But it was not *British Airways*' scene. She was built for fast passages in the less attractive waters of the world, and after we sold her, the new owner proved we had the concept right by completing a single-handed circumnavigation in her.

All this involvement convinced me that catamarans could be very fast and reliable seaboats and the real question was what size would be needed for an eighty-day circumnavigation? If one assumed that an average speed of 15 knots was required, a boat of at least 80 foot was the minimum necessary and, even then, there might not be sufficient margin of speed – 90 foot would be better.

All this was hypothetical as far as Peter and I were concerned because, with only five months before the French were due to sail, there was no time left to consider a new boat. If we wanted to have a shot at the record we had to depart with the French, since there was always the chance that either of them might reach the target. Competition would also provide a stimulus and it would make for a more interesting story. So we abandoned plans for a new boat. We needed to produce one which could be ready within four months and the only way to achieve this was to buy an existing boat and modify it as much as time and money allowed. A few discreet enquiries elicited that there were two large multihulls on the market, one in France but, much more interesting, Mike Birch's catamaran *Formula Tag*, which had sailed over 500 miles in one day during a transatlantic race, the sort of performance we had to aim for, was lying ashore near Newport, Rhode Island.

So Peter and I started to co-operate on a proposal, using an unnamed existing craft as the basis for our plans. We knew the craft would need a major refit and budgeted for this. We also expected to improve the accommodation, since none of the large multis was designed for more than an Atlantic crossing with a full crew. Crew comfort was important but secondary. If the money ran out we were quite prepared to live in a slum. We were not however prepared to sail slowly, so the bulk of the budget was allocated to the rig and sails. Our joint proposal was ready within two weeks and we put our heads together to select the potential sponsor targets.

Finding a sponsor is always an extremely difficult operation for major sailing projects because the costs involved limit the number of companies who can afford even to consider it. Added to this, larger companies tend on the whole to have more bureaucratic structures than their smaller counterparts, whose success has probably been due to a free-wheeling entrepreneur who makes decisions for himself. Bureaucracies do not usually encourage initiative and adventure, so those within such a structure seldom understand it. Even in a large adventurous company a spark is needed that will light the fire of interest in someone with authority who can see the benefits which could accrue from a rather specialised form of publicity. So although there were companies who could afford the project we had in mind, in practice many ruled themselves out. We identified our need as being for a company that was international or had aspirations to become international or one that was about to market a new product which could benefit from general news coverage, and they should want to market in Britain and New Zealand where Peter and I between us could provide the greatest impact.

Sponsorship has moved on from the days when someone gave a sailor £5,000 which bought a spinnaker and put the company's name on the side of the boat. This might have been billboard publicity, but the poster was tucked away at sea out of sight, not on the road out to Heathrow. The result was that few sponsors really got their money's worth from the investment. Such a lack of co-ordinated marketing did the sailors no good either, as when they went for sponsorship for their next project they had little to show in the way of media coverage to entice future backers.

In France the situation is far better as the television industry realised early on that sailing makes good and exciting programmes, with the result that for more than twenty years French sailors have been able to rely upon plenty of media exposure to encourage sponsors. In New Zealand Peter's Whitbread victory had made him a hero in a country which was producing many of the top international racing sailors and, whereas in Britain such a victory would have been yesterday's news within a few weeks, four years later Peter was still a national figure at home.

Whilst I approached two large companies based in Britain, Peter concentrated on New Zealand. One of the companies I contacted replied very speedily. It did not fit their current promotional plans. The other never did respond. This was shades of twenty-five years ago when I had been seeking sponsorship to attempt what was then described as impossible – to sail non-stop and alone around the world. I had written to fifty-two companies and received fifty-two noes in response, which forced me to sail unsponsored. Since sailing around the world in under eighty days was also seen as impossible I felt perversely encouraged by this similarity whilst I considered where to go next. Peter, in the meantime, was getting signs of interest from one of his candidates.

Whereas Britain could not produce a single challenger for the 1995 America's Cup, interest in New Zealand with its comparatively tiny population was considerable and Peter was heading up one of the syndicates. As a result he was in contact with a lot of companies and had a shrewd idea who to approach and he received an immediate interest from the New Zealand Apple and Pear Marketing Board which is responsible for selling the bulk of New Zealand's apples and pears all over the world. The business is large enough to warrant the chartering of close to a hundred reefer ships in an average year to carry the crop, mainly apples, to markets principally in Europe. It was our good fortune that they were in the process of introducing a new brand name, ENZA, and were looking for a means to get this before the public to back up their advertising campaign. To obtain a wider spread of publicity requires a news story that will be covered by the media and creating general news is not easy. This was why our project appealed to them. Around the world in eighty days is such a simple concept to grasp, whether or not you've read the original Jules Verne classic or seen the film. Indeed the magic time has already become a recognized target for globe-girdlers, maritime or otherwise.

We met in the London offices of the New Zealand Apple and Pear Marketing Board on the 17th September 1992 and as we left the meeting, which lasted an hour and a half instead of the planned half an hour, Peter turned to me and said, "How do you think that went?"

"If I were not so cautious I would say we have found a sponsor," I responded.

"Oh Lord, what have we got ourselves into!" Peter said, and we both laughed.

We were desperately short of time, only three and a half months remained, but things continued to happen very quickly. Peter had to go to New Zealand on America's Cup business and it was arranged he would meet the entire Marketing Board at their next meeting. Meanwhile I booked a weekend flight to Boston to take a quiet look at *Formula Tag*. We arranged to liaise as we each made progress.

My trip to Newport had all the elements of high farce. Peter Dunning, an old friend and known to anyone who has participated in the BOC Challenge or the Ostar single-handed races, collected me at the airport and took me to where the boat was lying. She looked neglected and forlorn. I collected the keys from a caretaker and explained I was looking at her on behalf of someone else – well, there was no point in alerting the owners to our interest as it would only put the price up.

The first thing to strike me was that she looked cut off at the stern since I last saw her, and closer investigation showed that her scoops were indeed lopped off. It had not improved her looks. I checked the hulls fore to aft, looked at the three crossbeams and in particular the connections to the hulls, and inspected the mast and rigging. Some of the winches were seized up, the electronic equipment seemed doubtful and the rigging very suspect, but the basic boat appeared solid. I could not find a structural crack anywhere. As I crawled out of the boat, congratulating myself on having managed to view her without being recognised, a mastless yacht came alongside the quay wall twenty yards away and a crane prepared to start stepping the mast. It was too late to hide. The boat was the new Open 60-footer *Cayote*, owned by American Mike Plant who picked me out immediately. My cover story was not that convincing, but I hoped he was so busy preparing his boat that he would not be too curious about what I was doing.

On returning to England I first phoned Nigel Irens, the designer and builder of *Tag*, and asked him whether he thought she was up to the task. Nigel is now probably the world's leading multihull designer with a string of successful boats to his credit and most of his work comes from the very competitive French market. *Tag* was built in Canada at an aircraft factory in 1984 and was one of the first boats to be built using the pre-impregnated technique, with kevlar and epoxy and a honeycomb core similar to that used in aircraft. In this she was way ahead of her time so, although now some eight years old, in construction terms she was still state of the art. When Peter and I next spoke I informed him the boat was basically sound but would need all the money we had allowed for her refit. He responded by telling me we were past the next hurdle, the Apple and Pear Marketing Board was calculating a budget and we would receive an official notification within a week. He agreed to contact the owner's brokers whilst I started preparations to get the boat over to Hamble for an urgent and speedy refit.

Signing the contract, though a vitally important detail, seemed to be just another bureaucratic item to be ticked off the long list. The boat was to be called *Enza New Zealand*, as this was the brand name the

Apple and Pear Marketing Board wished to promote. It took me a moment to appreciate that for the first time in my life I would not be sailing under a Red, White or Blue Ensign. But I told myself the New Zealand flag has the Union flag in it and I had always looked upon New Zealand rather as one looks upon another part of the United Kingdom, except at Twickenham, of course. So I did not feel too like a mercenary.

Time was rushing past. We were into the middle of October and the boat, although now ours, was still lying in America and needed a major refit. Fortunately, the French were beginning to move their estimated time of departure back. We heard that Titouan Lamazou's boat had been seriously damaged during trials and the liability was being investigated, so he would be unlikely to meet his December start date. Olivier de Kersuason was now rumoured to be leaving in early January, too, which confirmed we had a few days' remission if we were to start at the same time. Then we received news of another potential competitor to throw his hat into the ring, the likeable Frenchman Bruno Peyron. His boat was the well-proven catamaran *Jet Services*, holder of the transatlantic record with an average speed of more than 19 knots. Bruno was very competitive, highly experienced, plus he had a good boat. On previous form he looked more dangerous than de Kersuason and his boat was already in a shed being prepared, although he had not found a sponsor. Not only was the competition becoming more serious, our task was beginning to look more challenging as the days ticked away.

The press conference to announce the establishment of the Trophée Jules Verne was called for the 20th October. We debated avoiding it so as to go across to America sooner to collect the boat, but the sponsor ruled this was the right venue to announce our entry. Diaries were hastily rearranged and we flew to Paris that afternoon. The conference itself was a masterpiece of French organisation. In other words there was a plan, but it was not allowed to interfere with the evening's developments. Eventually we sat down, Peter at one end of the table and me at the other, separated by about three government ministers and two sailors, plus the inevitable chairman. The ministers spoke in turn, then Florence described her intentions and was followed by Titouan reporting on his progress. Neither had much to say, since

Florence was without a sponsor and Titouan was still arguing about the cause of his damage. At this point I was meant to make the surprise announcement but this was forgotten in the Gallic excitement and the floor was thrown open to questions. Twenty minutes into questions someone remembered we had something to say and turned to me. My speech was simple:

"New Zealand is known for the All Blacks (applause), and now it is going to become known world-wide for the Apple and Pear Marketing Board and the trade name Enza."

The audience looked polite and bemused. As I mentioned the two fruits Peter held up a sample of each in turn, just in case there was any confusion with my French pronunciation. I pressed on.

"We set off tomorrow to the United States to collect *Formula Tag*, which we bought last week. She will be sailed to Hamble for a refit and be renamed *Enza* after the sponsor. We shall be ready to sail early in the New Year."

The room went quiet. In the silence that followed, Bernard Moitessier, the well-known French sailor, leaned across towards Peter and picked up the pear he had been displaying. He produced a knife and calmly began to peel it. I hope he enjoyed it, it was probably French, as we had bought it that afternoon from a Parisian greengrocer!

2

A Match is Arranged

The crew who gathered in Newport at the weekend of the 23rd October 1992 was disparate. I had gone ahead and was soon joined by Peter and my nephew Rupert, who managed to attract immigration attention by declaring himself an out-of-work student! He had just finished taking a degree at Southampton and was still in that amusing anarchic state which universities seem to engender. Previously he had sailed with me in the Round Europe Race so had some knowledge of sailing catamarans. Don Wright, better known as Jaws, was one of Peter's *Steinlager 2* crew. He came up from the Caribbean to join us. Jean-François Coste, called simply Coste, was an old friend who had completed the Vendée Globe Challenge, a non-stop circumnavigation, and was invited because we recognised the advantages of having a Frenchman in the crew to handle the French press. This trip would be an opportunity for him to get acquainted with Peter and see whether they were compatible. Peter Lucas, who came along for the ride, runs a sailmaking company in Portchester, Hampshire. We all camped out at the long-suffering Peter Dunning's house whilst we prepared the boat.

The first task was to get the equipment working and, whilst Peter attended to that, I sourced wire and spliced up two heavy new backstays. The originals were of stainless steel, but one had lost its spring, a simple way of telling it was fatigued. We did not need anything 'racy' for the Atlantic crossing, just reliable, so three-inch-circumference galvanised steel wire rope did the trick, which gave me a happy day of splicing, as it was many years since I had handled anything so large. The sails were tatty but, with a few small repairs, we deemed them sufficient for the crossing, after which they would be discarded. We threw out a large number of unnecessary items, like an awning which had been used to cover the decks in the Caribbean, old sails and store items we would not need. The living areas received a scrub and we plugged some obvious holes in the structure which were probably welcomed in the tropics for ventilation but were less desirable in the North Atlantic in winter.

A vessel the size of a tennis court presents a problem when it comes to moving it around on dry land, and *Tag* was lying some forty feet from the water's edge. We hired a hundred-ton crane, not because the boat weighed that much, she weighed about ten tons, but because as the crane jibs out, or moves its head further from the cab, the weight it can safely lift decreases. We had been told the whole boat could be supported by her chain plates, the sturdy stainless steel plates firmly attached to the hull, and to which the rigging is fastened. In theory this was correct, of course, but the boat also needed to be steadied fore and aft. We solved this by putting the running backstays on to one lifting strop and a tackle from the forestay fitted to the forward beam. Then we held our breath as the crane took the weight at its maximum stretch. Slowly the weight came on. There is always creaking as this happens and we checked to ensure that nothing was actually being strained. Then up she went with the alarm bells ringing on the crane, indicating it was lifting at its limits. She had to be landed the other side of a security fence, unhitched and the crane moved before taking the weight again and finally lifting her into the water, but within a couple of hours she was floating – and no leaks! The mast followed quickly and there was our craft, afloat at last. Now the really heavy work began of loading and setting up the sails.

I don't think any of us was particularly happy at the thought of crossing the Atlantic this late in the year. It was only three years since I was dismasted by a storm in mid-Atlantic in November and had to sail 1,600 miles under a jury rig, and the sound of the waves breaking just before they crashed into my little boat is still a recurring nightmare. Nevertheless, there was no choice if we were to be ready in time. Even if we had all the alterations carried out in the United States, and the cost differential was frightening, we would still have to cross the

Atlantic before January to start with the others, so the sooner we pressed on with the voyage the better. The enforced sail would at least expose any serious defects and enable us to work out the necessary improvements.

We cleared the basin late in the afternoon of the 1st November. The channel down Narragansett Bay is well marked and as dusk fell we sailed out past Castle Point to the sea. The wind was a light north-easter, but even so, this was the first outing with an unknown boat, so we reduced sail to the third reef for the night. Once out past Brenton Light buoy (the famous tower, finish post for the Ostars, has been removed), the wind increased to between force 5 and 6 but backed a touch so we fine reached eastwards, passing Nantucket Light at 0330 hours the following morning. The weather forecasts were slightly worrying, as there was a storm 700 miles to our east, moving north-east, and a gale only 200 miles north, moving northwards. Good or bad was a high further north, moving east. We decided on an easterly course for the present. This gave us a comfortable aspect to the waves and followed the old passenger ship route which was designed to keep those leviathans clear of the ice zones, although this was not the season when bergs should be expected this far south. This route also kept us in the favourable current of the Gulf Stream.

We went into two watches, Peter with the other Peter and Jaws, and me with Rupert and Coste. Although we were in a hurry we made no effort to push the boat. The mast was old and worn, the sails no better, and everything screamed take it easy, so we did. When in doubt we reefed. On the second day we ran into a confused sea left behind by two weather systems and the wind eased as well, so progress slowed. Our day's runs were 182, 167, 101 and 230 miles, pretty pedestrian stuff, but the storms were moving away and another high coming in behind them straight over us. The immediate task was to cross the Atlantic, not set a new record.

The boat had two steering positions, one in each hull, and the gap between the hulls was bridged by netting. I had been concerned that it might seem somewhat disorientating to be steering from one side, rather like an aircraft carrier, but this was easier to adjust to than I imagined. The disadvantage of this side steering position was that the sea seemed to focus on it. In the confused seas we were encountering, every wave which broke over the boat, or reflected up from between the hulls, seemed to end up dumping itself over the poor helmsman. The wheels were set in small cockpits, about two foot deep and, to make matters worse, the water sloshed around one's feet until tiny cockpit drains allowed it to run overside. Whilst sloshing, it found its way down into the sleeping quarters through the numerous holes cut to allow various wires and controls access which we had yet to explore. Although we knew we could soon fix the leaks, the problem of protecting the helmsman was a real one.

We began to ask ourselves how efficient would the helmsman be if he was always wiping water out of his eyes, and could we afford to have this sort of distraction when sailing in excess of 25 knots? An instant reaction is essential if a squall catches the boat and starts to lift the weather hull clear of the water, as this is how a capsize starts. Then there was the question of exposure. For how long would the helmsman be able to remain at the helm lashed by spray in the Southern Ocean when the sea water temperature can reach just above freezing point?

I will admit to prejudice. All my cats had a central nacelle and Peter, coming from trimarans, was also used to steering from the middle hull. We began to discuss the advisability of adding a central pod to the boat. The disadvantage would be its weight, but the advantages would be a better protected steering position, and all the navigation and communication equipment could be in one place, instead of being shared between the hulls as at present. We could expect some compensatory weight savings too. At present the boat was set up so that all the sheets could be controlled from either hull, which led to duplication of many heavy items such as steering pedestals and winches. So we were soon examining our budget to see whether a central pod could be squeezed in and reaping a benefit of a sail before the refit, while we could still reassess our requirements and priorities.

On the 4th November the forecast was less attractive. One low was coming very close and another was due to combine with it, which implied an unpleasant time coming. Sure enough, the barometer began to fall and the wind increased to gale force from the south but soon veered south-west. We snugged right down and kept the speed below 12 knots. As the first depression passed to our north, the wind continued to veer and then ease, but then it backed south-westerly again and we knew the second depression was approaching. It too passed to our north, being reclassified as a storm as it went by. The wind reached a force 9 for a short time with a very heavy sea which we sailed through with just a fully reefed mainsail set. Thankfully, we were able to run before it. Although the speed was not fast, we still accelerated down the front of the larger waves and on one occasion cannoned into the back of the wave in front. I had been standing leaning against the aft beam talking to Jaws when this happened once and the sudden deceleration caused me to lose my grip and tumble forward. Fortunately, the boat levelled out before I rolled into the main beam. This is a regular hazard with lightweight craft in large seas but my antics amused the others and no harm was done.

Although conditions were rough and wet the boat was handling them extremely well. Peter wanted to know whether catamarans usually handled like this and I could honestly say that all mine had. Trimarans apparently have some difficulty with the outer floats as the weather one bashes into the seas in bad conditions and creates a very unpleasant motion, apart from placing a huge strain on the structure. He was finding the big cat's motion reassuring and I was impressed at the ease with which we were able to manage her. Not all the crew found it that easy of course. Coste was in his element, his experience showed, but when I told Rupert to take over the helm from him, we were running before some very large waves which required full concentration and he looked a bit apprehensive, which was not surprising in the circumstances. He coped very well, but was visibly relieved when I suggested that I take the wheel after an hour. Coste, who had been watching proceedings, just grinned and muttered something about *bon expérience*!

People don't fully appreciate the enormous strains which are created on a multihull's rigging. Because they cannot heel over and ease the weight of wind in the sails when hit by a squall, the rig has to take the full strain. Sometimes this is sufficient to lift the weather hull out of the water, so the main shrouds have to be at least strong enough to take the weight of the boat. Our three-inch wires had a theoretical breaking strain of twenty-seven tons, but even so they stretched to the point where we had taken up all the slack in the rigging screws.

Stainless steel will stretch less, of course, but it will work harden over time and the leeward shrouds are always slopping about on a multi which provides the movement to accelerate this hardening process. I have had a two-and-a-half-inch circumference stainless steel shroud part after just two Atlantic crossings which deposited the mast into the sea off Land's End and undermined my faith in the material ever since. Here was a decision we would have to make. We needed strength and stamina from the shrouds, so we began to give serious consideration to using man-made fibre ones on the grounds they would stretch less, also save a great deal of weight and reduce the pitching moment.

Because I had always lived in a centre pod in my boats, a surprising factor, and one we had not anticipated, was the tremendous noise created in the hulls by the sound of water rushing past at high speed. It was rather like standing in an underground train with waves crashing into the sides. Speech was difficult and sleep a problem as the racket made it hard to drop off. Since none of us had brought ear plugs, the best we could do was smother our ears with a pillow. Part of the trouble was undoubtedly due to apprehension. The noise made it sound as if the boat was moving dangerously quickly and one could not help thinking that at any moment a hull might be lifted out of the water and those on deck not react quickly enough to save us from capsizing. Actually, the sound of water should have been reassuring. When it stopped was the time to worry!

Meals were cooked in a sort of rota, everyone taking a turn. I awaited Coste's contribution with relish, as my years of sailing with the French had taught me that they took a far greater interest in creating meals in testing conditions than we do. We were not disappointed. He produced a superb spaghetti. My specialities are stews and curries, but both need time and are improved by being made the day before, which is just not possible in a small galley with limited facilities. The best I could do was prepare the evening meal in the morning on the day it was to be consumed.

During the trip I kept in contact with friends in Newport who between them operate a maritime amateur radio network. For some time they had been trying to call Mike Plant, in *Cayote*, who planned to compete in the Vendée Globe Challenge but had never arrived in France. In his last contact he reported a complete electrical failure which would have prevented him using the radio thereafter. More seriously, this also meant that he would not have an automatic pilot to steer the boat and so would have to heave to when he needed sleep. I found that I could steer about eighteen hours a day when the same thing happened while I was sailing alone around the world, but I could then balance the boat for the other six hours. *Cayote* was a 60-foot Open class thoroughbred, and I doubted very much that Mike would get her to balance. He was now overdue, beyond even the time he should have taken if he had to steer fifteen hours a day, and there was growing concern for his safety. The search and rescue authorities had checked out a number of emergency beacon transmissions with reconnaissance aircraft but nothing had been sighted near any of the transmission points. The modern EPIRB operates on 406 mega-hertz and its signal, which can be identified individually, is picked up by a satellite system jointly operated by the United States and Russia. So far nothing recognisable had come through on this system. As our course passed close to Mike's anticipated track we were asked to keep a lookout. We saw nothing, except a brown Igloo cold bucket which might have come from anywhere, and conditions were too rough to stop to pick it up. A subsequent search found *Cayote* lying upside down with her keel missing. There was no sign of Mike. The sea had claimed another good single-hander.

The weather continued messy for us. Force 6–8's every other day with a period of light stuff and sloppy seas in between characterised the whole crossing. We did have two better days when the sea's state allowed us to hold on to sail and during these we made 298 and 325 miles respectively. This was nowhere near what was required for the Jules Verne but good enough to show the potential was there. Soon we were picking up the weather forecasts from the BBC on long wave and then, as we reached soundings (when the sea shallows to a hundred fathoms, the limit of the old deep-sea lead line), we started to sight fishing craft, all signs of nearing home, and just after midnight on the 15th November we made our landfall on Start Point. Four hours later we raised Portland Bill and surged in towards the Solent. The last time Peter and I sailed through these waters together had been at the end of the Whitbread Race in 1978 aboard *Heath's Condor* as we came in to take line honours for the final leg. Then there was a full gale behind, this time we were becalmed off the chalky teeth of the Needles, extending from the western end of the Isle of Wight. In light winds we cruised slowly through the Solent towards the Hamble River where a launch took us alongside a pontoon at Hamble Point Marina. It had taken us fifteen days to cross the Atlantic, not fast, but the boat arrived in one piece, which was the objective. Now the yard had seven weeks to complete a major refit, a Herculean task.

Whilst we could feel pleased that, so far at any rate, things had gone to plan, there was one disappointment as far as I was concerned. Coste had decided that he could not accompany us on the actual circumnavigation. His reason was one of basic communication difficulties. He and I could communicate easily. Having often sailed with the French I have a good nautical vocabulary in their language and Jean-François's English is far from bad. However, Peter and Jaws had no French at all and he found their New Zealand accents hard to understand, especially inside a noise-battered hull. This had led to difficulties in appreciating exactly what they meant, which was frustrating and potentially dangerous. I was extremely sorry. Not only is Coste an old friend, he is a very good sailor and would have been invaluable for improving our reporting within France, not to mention improving my French conversation.

Nigel Irens, as the original designer of the boat, was brought into our deliberations early on when considering what changes to make to improve performance. Both Peter and I felt the length should be increased. The original length had been 85 feet, but the scoops were removed when the overall length for racing multihulls was reduced to 80 feet. Not only did the boat look stunted without them but there was also noticeable transom drag, when the water passing the boat is held up behind the transom instead of flowing away freely. We had already agreed a central nacelle was essential, but it had to be designed and engineered to take the strains which would be imposed on it. Introducing a nacelle would mean we could strip out the two side steering cockpits, thus providing greater headroom in the crew sleeping quarters below and we could then do something about the leaks and the noise.

The performance of a multihull is extremely weight-sensitive and weight is probably the most important factor to affect speed. If craft have the same shape and sail area, they should travel at the same speed, but the moment weight is added to one, it is asking its engine, the sails, to achieve more output if it is to maintain the same speed. Unless the sail area is increased this will not happen and performance will drop off. So we were extremely conscious of the need to reduce weight wherever possible. Adding the nacelle was an addition to our all up weight but one we felt would be justified by the better control over the boat.

As compensation for the additional weight of the nacelle, however, we decided to throw away the existing aluminium mast and replace it with a much lighter one made from carbon fibre by Carbospars. The material used was M40J high modulus carbon. This costs four times as much as basic carbon fibre, but has twice the modulus, an engineering term that relates to the stiffness of the material. Because it is stiffer, less is required compared with a standard material. Carbon has a huge tensile strength along its length, something like twenty times stronger than stainless steel or aluminium, but this strength is only available when the material is used properly. The fibre must be set up in a multi-directional laminate in a resin matrix and for our new spar some sixty-eight per cent of the fibre used was laid along the axis which provides the main load-bearing fibre. The balance was laid off axis to stabilise the spar section and take the torsional loads. In this configuration the laminate was three times stronger than aluminium for the same weight or, put another way, could be built to a third of the equivalent weight of aluminium. In practice this is not possible as other factors have to be taken into account, such as wall buckling.

Nevertheless the weight saving was considerable and, when combined with kevlar rigging, the total mast and rigging weight was reduced to 1,600 pounds, half the old mast's weight or, as Damon Roberts, Carbospars' Managing Director (to whom I am indebted for the technical background), descriptively put it, the equivalent of saving the weight of a mini car forty-five feet up the mast! This had the enormous benefit of reducing the pitching moment and the righting lever required to keep the boat upright. A carbon fibre mast is not cheap, but this decision was probably the most cost-effective change we made. The lighter mast meant lighter rigging loads, which in turn meant lighter rigging and all its attendant fittings. We took full advantage of this bonus but instead of actually decreasing the size and strength of the running rigging we increased the mast height by four feet from ninety-eight to 102 feet overall height and we introduced a much larger sail plan, allowing us to increase the horsepower.

We also ordered a carbon fibre boom, and an experienced yacht designer, David Alan-Williams, who was going to join the crew, suggested that sail handling would be a great deal easier and safer if we put a platform along the top to provide access, an idea for which we were to be very grateful. Despite this addition, the new boom weighed only two-thirds of the old aluminium one. To control the sail when reefing, lazy jacks were fitted. These are lines which run from mast to boom either side of the sail and prevent it flopping on to the deck when it is being lowered.

There were two companies in the UK we could have used for the refit but we chose Carbospars because their works were at Hamble Point, where the sheds were large enough to take the boat, and it was easy for us to travel there and keep an eye on things. Normally it is not cost effective to flood a job with manpower to hasten its completion, the workmen get in each others way or are held up waiting to use machinery, but, fortunately, our craft was so big that once she was under cover it was possible for a small army to tackle the tasks we had in mind without mutual interference.

There was so much to do and far too little time to do it, but optimism had got us this far and everybody associated with the project was enthusiastic. To hurry things along Nigel came up from Devon three days a week to work on the drawings for the modification of his design. We had already determined to have more hull length and now considered ways of achieving this. One would have been to cut the hulls amidships and introduce a new section. But we ruled this out on the grounds of cost, time and an old-fashioned prejudice against introducing a potential weakness in the middle of a boat which would have to survive the Southern Ocean. We confirmed extensions at the sterns instead and gained five feet this way.

The design for a pod (later christened the godpod by the crew!), initially loosely based upon a *British Oxygen* sketch I gave Nigel, went through an interesting series of modifications. This structure was held between the main and after beam on two foam composite beams in glass with carbon fibre reinforcing to provide the strength to take the tension exerted when we loaded a sheet to haul in a sail. We were to learn that easing a mast runner or sheet when they were under a high load created a huge creaking noise which was unnerving until one became accustomed to it.

Initially the pod was drawn rather low and narrow but as each of us popped into the office the height rose slightly and the beam increased. The final drawing gave no standing room but comfortable seating, bunks for Peter and myself, a chart table and two settees. A dome was fitted to the top to enable us to see out and give some light. Into this small area was jammed the radio, Satcom C satellite communication equipment, which gives almost instant contact with the shore by telex, all the Autohelm instruments, the Garmin GPS, weatherfax and the controls for the battery-charging generators. The pod narrowed to nothing at the front but widened out into a full-size cockpit behind the entrance hole – doorway would not be a good description since no door existed! The roof of the pod was extended aft over the first two feet of the cockpit to provide shelter for the watch on duty when they were not steering. There is no point in leaving people in the open, unnecessarily exposed to spray and a high wind chill factor, as it only decreases efficiency.

The cockpit itself was relatively simple, containing just the steering wheel and its pedestal, and winches for sail control with the Autohelm array of instrumentation, including two powerful automatic pilots. The inclusion of these had entailed a change in the steering to hydraulic rams from the rather stiff cables which saw us across the Atlantic and were a real improvement. The criticism levelled at hydraulics is that they do not provide a feedback of rudder pressure to the helmsman, but in my experience this has never mattered with the big cats, since you are steering by instruments the whole time anyway. What hydraulic steering does give is positive and easy control.

Our electrical requirement was to be considerably heavier than the boat previously needed, and since we were dependent upon it not only for all communications but for the instrumentation and filming as well, we could not afford to take risks with our ability to keep the batteries charged. The boat had one diesel generator just astern of the living quarters on the starboard side when we collected her. This was far from convenient as it was noisy and fumes, both from the exhaust and the diesel oil, inevitably penetrated into the living quarters. Once we reached Hamble this was removed as it was deemed untrustworthy on account of its appearance, indeterminate age and lack of a history. It was replaced by two new ones which were given military specification alternators which had a second set of coils in them so that if one broke down we could still obtain a charge from the other. One was placed in each hull behind the aft beam so they were clear of the crew's quarters, and this enabled us to charge whichever tack we were on since the leeward one would always have its cooling water inlets in the sea. The windward hull was often clear of the water, especially when we were sailing fast. We considered backing the generators with solar cells but chose windmill generators instead. They were placed on special individual masts right at the rear of each hull. Though it all ended up being a net increase in weight, this was an area where reliability was paramount, not just for our comfort and safety but for the sponsor's PR needs as well.

Water is heavy, and if everyone were allowed a gallon a day for all purposes it would mean carrying 560 gallons, which weighs more than two tons. It is possible to augment fresh water from rainfall. Indeed I spent eight months at sea living entirely on this source during my solo non-stop circumnavigation, but it is an unreliable source of supply. We preferred to install a water-maker in each hull which filtered clear drinking water from sea water. The performance varied considerably depending upon the temperature. It was better in warmer water. But we were never short. We usually kept six gallons spare and topped up the ready-use container as necessary.

This water supply became more critical once we decided to choose dried food as the basis of our diet. McDougalls do a whole range of menus which come in ten-person packs about the size of a pint mug. Add 1.5 litres of water, soak for an hour and then bring to the boil and the meal is ready to eat. When compared with the weight of the equivalent tinned food here was another enormous saving. These meals turned out to taste much better than expected and we were never undernourished or hungry, in fact most of us put on weight. The task of packing the food into weekly boxes fell to Peter's wife Pippa with a group of friends, and they were packed so that all we had to do was take three large plastic boxes to the galley each week. The menus did not vary much, although there was some slight recognition of the different requirements of warmer and colder climates. The cold weather individual Christmas puddings were especially popular.

It may seem to be a contradiction to put water ballast tanks into a craft where so much effort is being made to keep weight to a minimum, but the aft ends of each hull were sealed off and electric water pumps fitted so that they could be filled and emptied quickly if necessary. In some conditions additional water *can* be of use. For example, if we were sailing with a strong wind and wanted to keep as much sail set as possible, one method of providing increased stability would be to add weight to the windward hull. The BOC Open 60-foot monohulls have fitted wing tanks for twelve years to benefit from this principle and the Whitbread 60s have recently copied the idea. We also thought there might be occasions when it would be sensible to add weight to one of the hulls to keep it from leaping out of the water. The other reason was that in really rough weather there is an advantage in having greater displacement, so long as the structure is sufficiently strong. The greater weight means the boat is not thrown about quite so much by the large waves and it can make the difference between the boat being flipped upside down or remaining upright. Should the tanks, which would hold three tons each, prove insufficient, we planned to add sea water into each hull amidships where the dagger boards were located, but this would be a desperate measure.

Unlike most conventional yachts, multihulls have watertight subdivisions. Thus if a hull is holed only about a quarter of its length should get flooded. The boats need to be savagely handled or mortally damaged before they are in danger of sinking. These bulkheads also provide another safety factor against the worst risk in a multihull, the danger of capsizing. When a strong squall hits a monohull she will heel before the additional weight of wind and may even go on to her side. The moment the pressure is released, however, the weight of the keel will bring her back upright again. Since a multihull has no keel, when a squall hits the boat she accelerates and if she cannot dispose of the surplus power this way, she will begin to lift the weather hull. If the wind is sufficient, the hull will rise right up until the boat goes on to her side. At this point the weight of the mast is being dragged down by gravity and the boat will only be stable again when she is upside down. A large multihull requires a dockyard crane to right her, and this is an item in rather short supply at sea! In these circumstances the crew are pretty safe, provided they have survived the initial capsize, because the watertight subdivision means that the boat will float around almost indefinitely. All large multis have entry ports in the hulls that allow exit or access when the boat is capsized. In *Enza*'s case these hatches were in the galley and WC compartments and, since they had perspex windows, they gave some light and a view from within the hulls. We fitted additional hatches to the two generator compartments so that we could get at these and the water-makers in such an emergency. Life would not be luxurious in an upside-down *Enza*, but at least the crew would survive until rescuers arrived.

The choice of crew was fundamental to the project and we agreed a crew of six should be sufficient. This would mean three watches of two when conditions were light and two of three when more labour was required on deck. Sailing any craft requires teamwork and compatibility of a very high degree. We needed to find highly competent sailors, experienced in long-distance ocean passages, who could be relied upon to undertake the myriad tasks involved in sailing a boat, from steering to sailmaking, cooking to splicing, cleaning to overhauling a generator, understanding electronics to sail-trimming, to name just a few. There are plenty of able sailors about, but we wanted to choose people who were absolutely reliable, so this restricted us to those we had sailed with before or who had unimpeachable recommendations.

Don Wright was already included. A batchelor of thirty-five, he had sailed with Peter in two Whitbreads aboard *Ceramco* and *Steinlager 2*. He has a nice cheery disposition which make him good to work with. Peter had said I would like him and he was right. The nickname 'Jaws' was due to his insatiable hunger and went back to an occasion when the cook had thrown some dough overboard and Don leaped after it and caught it almost before it hit the water. He was able to eat enormous quantities of food and whilst he might not hear a shouted order to change a headsail, he never missed a whispered suggestion that we have a cup of tea. You could say it when he was seventy feet away and the boat was hissing through the water and he would return to the cockpit immediately with his happy grin and say, "Did someone mention a cuppa?" Reliable, sometimes difficult to wake, competent, good company, Jaws was to be my watchmate when we sailed in January and I thoroughly enjoyed his company.

Our next choice was David Alan-Williams because he had been in *Condor* in the 1977 Whitbread and sailed with Peter when they both crewed aboard *Burton Cutter* in the first Whitbread in 1973. David had qualified as a naval architect in 1977 and was the in-house architect for Contessa Yachts for six years. More recently he had worked independently, being responsible for the design of *Steinlager 1*. When asked if he would like to join us, he said yes before he even thought about it. We were delighted. David, or DAW as the New Zealanders insist on calling him, has sailed in three Admiral's Cup boats, two Whitbreads and countless other races. His knowledge of boat design and building, which was to be so important, was immense and he is very congenial generally. He started co-operating with Nigel Irens almost immediately and shared the heavy workload.

Paul Standbridge came to us highly recommended, since neither Peter nor I had sailed with him before. After an early engineering training he took to sailing as a profession and had been working hard ever since. He was one of Lawrie Smith's watch leaders aboard *Rothmans* in what was his third Whitbread Race, having gained a reputation as a first-class bowman both in the Whitbreads and the *White Crusader* America's Cup challenge in Fremantle. Having been bowman aboard both *Frigate* and *Yeoman XX* in two Admiral's Cups myself, I was more than interested, and perhaps a little prejudiced, but the depth of experience, not only of flat-out round-the-cans racing, but also hard ocean competition, made Paul exactly the sort of person we were seeking. We found that those who recommended him had not exaggerated his abilities and he was easy company aboard with a delightful and occasional wacky sense of humour.

Ed Danby had previously sailed with both Peter and me – with me as a youngster, with Peter aboard *Lion New Zealand* in 1985 – then with Grant Dalton in *Fisher and Paykel* in the 1989 Whitbread and as crew in two America's Cup boats, *Lionheart* and *Kiwi Magic*. He is one of those sailors with the sort of voice you have no problem hearing clearly in the middle of a noisy operation in a storm. A distinct advantage in those circumstances, less so if you are trying to get to sleep. Ed is instant action, and wastes no time pausing to consider whether there are alternative ways of doing a job, which can be a disadvantage. But he likes nothing better than to be fiddling about making some little extra improvement for the boat.

Finally, because filming at sea is time consuming, we decided to increase the crew by one professional cameraman. Both Peter and I have used cameras before and I flatter myself I can hold one more steadily than most because I am used to focusing on the horizon when using a sextant. But neither of us had the background knowledge of how a film is made and what edits best for a popular viewing market. So we resolved to take a cameraman whose primary task was to film. Even if we struck an emergency he was expected to film, not help. An additional person was a weight penalty, of course. However the sponsor was not putting up the money just so we could have an exciting sail, he wanted to see it, and that meant TV. George Johns had done some filming aboard a boat with David Alan-Williams, who spoke well of him, and our suspicions that this was the beginning of a Welsh Tafia within the crew proved to be unfounded!

You cannot get a true impression of the looks of a boat whilst she is in a shed, but when *Enza* emerged gleaming in her newly painted livery she showed little resemblance to the rather battered lady who entered eight weeks earlier. Only when the mast was stepped, though, was the most noticeable feature exposed – a very dramatic rake. It was racy, in fact to those accustomed to normal racing rigs it looked over-racy. The true reason was not one of technical innovation or a desire to have the boat appear extreme, as many suspected, but far more prosaic. We needed to bring the centre of effort of the rig aft and this was the only way to do it. The addition of five feet on length aft meant that the centre of lateral resistance had moved about half that distance aft. So to maintain the balance of the boat the centre of effort had to come aft as well. This normally means moving the mast but this we could not do unless we moved the main beam on which it was stepped, an expensive operation. To avoid this we adopted the cheaper and easier method of raking the mast backwards to achieve the same effect. The result was certainly eye-catching but the handling ability of the boat was unchanged.

By the New Year our schedule was running a few days late but

Carbospars had performed miracles in achieving so much in just over two months. We had intended to launch on the 7th January 1993, but we did not step the new mast until the 9th and then appalling weather forced further delays on the programme. We finally had the christening on the 11th with the boat still perched on trolleys at the top of the slipway. The storms which prevented us from launching also doubled the time required to do tasks, and a particularly high tide that flooded the entire works area at Hamble Point caused even further hold-ups. *Enza* was safe but the equipment store in one of the sheds was flooded. Ed commandeered a dinghy and floated a lot of the stores to safety, which later cost us £40 in repairs to the dinghy. On balance we considered this good value for money!

It was galling to wait but the winds were not favourable for sailing to France or setting out on the actual voyage, so they were thwarting our French competitors as well. We were all too acutely conscious that we still had trials to do, whereas the French were ready, as far as we knew. If a favourable weather pattern developed before we tested the boat properly, we might well see the competition depart and leave us to wait until the next weather pattern came along, which might be weeks ahead. We could only pray the others had their own delays so we could all start together. There were two aspects to the competition, just as there had been twenty-four years before racing for the *Sunday Times* Golden Globe Trophy – the race to be first and the race to be fastest. The prime objective, however, was to be first to get round in less than eighty days. We expected the race to be tight, since the boats appeared pretty evenly matched, so if one boat sailed early it would have an immediate lead and the pressure would be on the others to catch up. The last thing we wanted was to start under that sort of strain.

Before we could leave there was one symbolic gesture we had to make: dine at the Reform Club in London, where Phileas Fogg and his faithful servant Passepartout started on their journey in Jules Verne's book. A small group of us travelled to London for the occasion, hosted by John Owen and Oliver Stanley, the latter having crossed the Atlantic with me ten years before. The dark panelling and deep leather chairs were a marked contrast to the accommodation we would enjoy for the next three months. We wondered whether we could return in a similar time to the resourceful Mr Fogg.

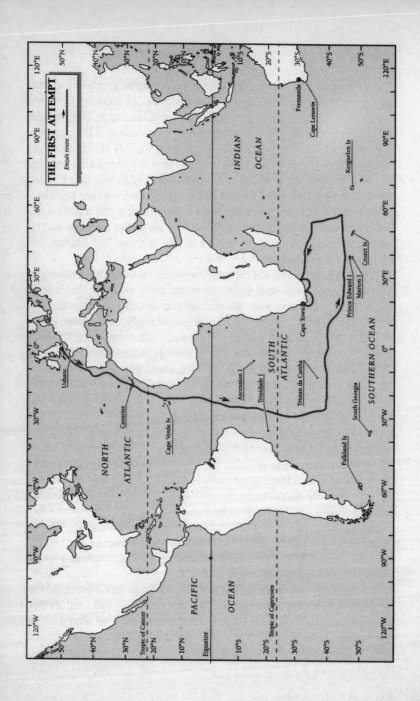

THE FIRST ATTEMPT

— Enza's route

3

First Attempt

There was a sense of urgency about the trials which took place around the Solent in mixed but generally cold weather in January. Each day for a week we went out, taking the various manufacturers and installers so everything could be checked and checked again. For all who came along it was a great thrill to be aboard when we were able to open up. The speeds were impressive. *Enza* was a far more sparkling craft than *Tag* ever was and there was no question that the modifications dramatically improved both performance and handling. It was easy to reach to 20 knots, with 26 being the best amidst a welter of spray, which gave everyone an exciting ride and did much for our confidence.

The start and finish line for the Jules Verne Trophy was set between the Ushant lighthouse just off Brest in Brittany and the Lizard lighthouse in Cornwall so it tactfully straddles the English Channel. Both points are major marks for shipping, but the bias favours the French end of the line by nearly a hundred miles, as Ushant is that much closer to Cape Finisterre in Spain at the south-western end of the Bay of Biscay, the first turning mark. In fact there is no ideal start line which lies perpendicular to the course for Cape Finisterre, unless the French end were to be moved towards Cherbourg and the English end out to the Bishop Rock off the Scilly Islands. Since the bias could not be ignored, it was obviously sensible to leave from the Ushant end so we decided to sail to Brest when we were ready and wait there for a suitable weather window.

As we ran out of items to be adjusted or changed during the trials, the focus of attention switched ever more to the forthcoming weather. The wrong pattern at the start might cost at least two days and those would be very hard to retrieve. The rules stated quite clearly that no outside assistance was allowed and we interpreted this to mean that no special weather and routing information could be supplied for an individual contestant during the race. However, we considered this did not prohibit taking advice before the start, so we contacted a routier in the USA, Bob Rice, and asked him to watch for a suitable weather window to blast us from Ushant across the Bay of Biscay and down the Portuguese coast until we could pick up the north-east trade winds. We discovered later that the French had interpreted the no outside assistance rule quite differently. Bizarrely, they did not consider routing information was outside assistance and both craft received daily instructions from specialists ashore. The advantage is obvious. It is not possible to carry all the equipment to receive every source of weather information aboard the boat, nor is it viable to access weather computers ashore. Even if it was, and this would mean additional weight, electricity requirement and costs, it still takes time to analyse by crew who are concentrating on sailing the boat to the maximum of their ability and run a tiring watch system. A shore-based specialist can analyse all the information and pass on the conclusions to the boat, so the crew can focus totally on sailing.

Bob Rice's long-term prognosis was that we might have a window about the third week in January but it was narrow and at this stage showed only slight indications of the continuous northerlies we needed to propel us from Ushant right into the north-east trade winds. He doubted it was good enough. There was a chance of a better one a week later, although weather forecasts are a very perishable commodity. Peter and I watched intently as the systems developed. Although we obviously needed favourable winds now, we also wanted to be round Cape Horn before the end of March, as winter in the Southern Ocean is no place for any boat, particularly a multihull. The first window did provide a northerly of moderate strength but it did not last. Olivier de Kersuason in *Charal*, who by refusing to accept the official Jules Verne Association rules was proceeding independently and had therefore put himself under pressure to be different, took this chance and made a reasonable crossing of the bay but slowed once round the corner. By sailing early de Kersuason had started his personal eighty-day clock ticking, even if he should have waited for a better system. Still, he was building a lead and, if he did speed up, there was no way anyone else would beat him for the first to circumnavigate in under eighty days. The heat was now on for ourselves and for *Commodore*, as Bruno's *Jet Services* had become. Sadly, Titouan had not managed to get his huge monohull repaired and was not joining in this year. We watched de Kersuason's early progress and relaxed somewhat as his speeds failed to reach the average required and, as if realising that he was not doing very well, he went off the air. We could not be certain we would get a better window of course, but the time had come to position ourselves in Brest just in case. The final stores were loaded on the 27th January 1993.

I have been a smoker since 1964, apart from six months when I gave up to win a bet with Nigel Dempster. I was keen to stop again because it is a pretty silly habit and hard to beat. This voyage seemed to be the ideal opportunity and in eighty days I hoped to get over the pangs completely. If the British have a gambling compulsion the virus appears to have carried to New Zealand as the moment he heard of my good intentions the sponsor's representative, Brian Aitken, bet me I couldn't manage it, which was exactly the incentive I needed. The stake was agreed as a dozen bottles of Bollinger and the bet started when we departed on the actual voyage. Since I was not sure what my reaction might be to the sudden deprivation, I decided to stop as we left Hamble so that, if I found it totally unbearable, at least I could buy sufficient supplies of cigarettes in Brest before we finally set off. Before we cast off from Hamble Point Marina at 1040 hours on the 28th January 1993 I smoked a final cigarette and then, seeing Brian on the bridge of a following motor boat as we sailed out through the Solent, I ostentatiously threw my remaining cigarettes into the sea one by one. Now, if I had any shame at all, I really had to quit.

The first two days as we sailed across to Brest were busy ones, but I still caught myself reaching into my pockets for a smoke every so often. Then the interval between thoughts of smoking began to lengthen and when we arrived in Brest I was sure that I would win. Brian, who flew over to join us, saw what for him were negative signs and wisely laid off half the bet with Peter. Not for nothing is Brian a salesman! To put me under pressure they placed a carton of cigarettes aboard. The idea behind this was not only to lure me into smoking again so I would lose the bet, but also to charge me a fortune for each one when I was desperate. This was a tactical error as few smokers can manage on two or three a day, so I knew if I succumbed to temptation I would not only lose the bet, but then be obliged to go through all the suffering again when their stocks ran out within ten or twenty days. But I decided not to mention this. There was talk of putting a cigarette in my mouth whilst I was asleep in order to take incriminating photographs, which I took as a sign of increasing desperation on their part and it gave my confidence a boost. Naturally, I thought I coped remarkably well, but one of the crew, when asked later what it had been like, stated I was very scratchy for the first ten days of withdrawal symptoms. I would recommend a long voyage on a cigaretteless ship to anyone who wants to stop. I have not smoked since nor felt any desire to.

We did not escape from the Solent without incident. One of the press boats, closing from the beam, suddenly lost control and motored straight at our side. For an awful moment we saw all the preparations and work being lost as it made to carve into the port hull. Fortunately partial control was recovered at the last minute and the engines went astern, but not before it came close enough for its bow to smash one of the stanchions. It was an unpleasantly close shave, as a few more inches ahead would have been disastrous, we would have had to return for repairs and missed the next opportunity to sail.

The weather in the Channel was lousy – rain, poor visibility and the wind from the south-west. We tacked down the Channel, thankful for radar and GPS (Global Positioning System), a satellite-based navigation system which gives a position every three seconds to within 250 feet accuracy. The system is US military in origin, and degraded for civilian use, but anyone who has struggled in poor visibility with a sextant desperately trying to find a position after days without sights, greets GPS with delight. A day into the crossing the wind came round to the north-east and dropped, and we slopped our way slowly towards the Canal du Four between Ushant Island and the mainland. It was not until 0345 on the 30th that we anchored off Camaret, outside the entrance channel to Brest and awaited a tow boat which arrived seven hours later. We secured astern of *Commodore* in Moulin Blanc Marina at Brest just after midday.

This was the first chance to see part of the competition who two years before as *Jet Services* had set the transatlantic sailing record with the incredible time of 6 days, 13 hours and 3 minutes. She was low in the water compared with us and had her controls in either hull as we had before the refit. They obviously found these exposed, as fragile-looking screens were erected outboard of each cockpit to protect the helmsman. It still looked vulnerable but they retained this arrangement as they believed our central nacelle system put the on-duty watch at risk from being trapped in the event of a capsize. We suspected they had not seen the escape hole we had built into the bottom of our pod! Their crew were professionals with plenty of Atlantic crossings but no forays into the Southern Ocean, whereas we all had this experience. They gave the impression of not being ready or not wanting to be ready, and the negative attitude was emphasised when one of them commented that the eighty-day record was not possible in boats so small. There was a distinct lack of fire about them then, but it was a miserable day and they were in their home port preparing to say goodbye to families and friends, whereas we were already emotionally underway.

We had a brief discussion with Bruno about a twice daily radio schedule for mutual safety and talked about the weather for setting off. The French routiers declared it would be best to leave next midday, but Bob Rice told us to go at 0600 hours if we wanted to get the best out of the system. Six hours may not seem much but during that short time the wind might change considerably and we were not prepared to risk missing the connection of the systems at Cape Finisterre. A little old lady on the pontoon asked me indignantly why we refused to sail together, as if to say didn't we know the French were the only people who understood meteorology. She became quite cross when we said we preferred to rely on our routier. Frankly, we thought Bruno was delaying to allow the television to cover his departure. Brian Aitken put no pressure on Peter and me to suit the media. His view was that the important thing was to beat the record, and we were left to make the decisions on sailing matters. We were lucky it was Brian backing us and not some all-knowing PR guru who could have jeopardised the project for a few column inches.

The tow boat came alongside at 0100 hours and we began the journey to the start. There had been rumours that no tow boats would be available until daylight, a move designed to ensure we sailed simultaneously with Bruno, but this drama did not materialise. The wind was forecast to be from the north-east at 15 knots, but due to rise. It was as good a forecast as we could hope for. The atmosphere aboard was quiet and businesslike, there was no great excitement, we were just getting on with the job. We crossed the start line on the 31st January 1993 at 0551 and 58 seconds on starboard tack, gybed within five minutes, and set a spinnaker. We were off. Around the world, without outside assistance, leaving the Cape of Good Hope, Cape Leeuwin in Australia and Cape Horn, to the north and all in less than eighty days.

A multihull does not sail at her best when close to the wind. In fact the performance rarely outdoes a monohull's. Maximum performance for a multihull comes when she is off the wind or sailing free, which means the wind is coming more from behind than from the front of the boat. The big square-riggers could not sail very close to the wind. Perhaps 65°–70° was the best they could expect (a modern racing yacht can get to between 25°–30°, so they chose routes which enabled them to reach their destinations with the wind, as near as possible, from the beam or behind them. So the route was simple. The old sailing ship routes, which are well tried and documented, would most likely provide the course to produce the maximum speed from *Enza*.

The traditional sailing route from Europe to Australia and back again starts with a beat out westward against the south-westerly winds of the North Atlantic until turning south to pick up the *nortada*, a northerly wind, which blows down the coast of Portugal. This extends into the north-east trade winds of the North Atlantic which continue almost as far as the inter-tropical convergence zone (ITCZ) just north of the equator. This is the area of the infamous doldrums, light winds or calms interspersed with occasional squalls, and very hot. Any route plan must allow for a slow passage at this point until the south-easterly trades of the South Atlantic are met. These winds, discovered by the Portuguese in the fifteenth century, are part of the anti-clockwise circulation round a large high pressure area in the South Atlantic. The direct route towards Cape Town appears the best way to

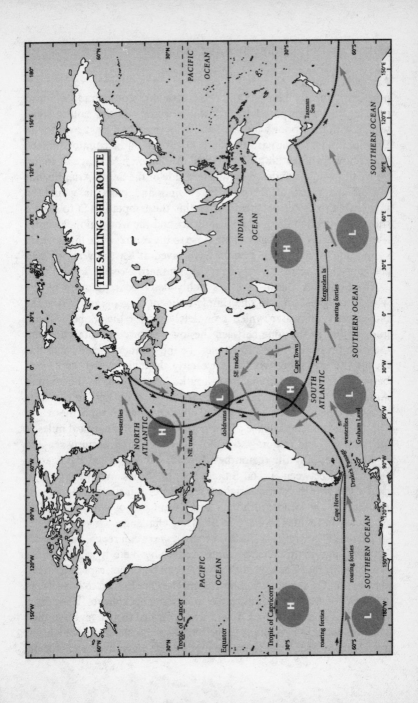

Australia from this point but in ocean sailing the shortest route is not necessarily the quickest one and this is straight into the trade wind, so once again we proposed to follow the lessons of the sailing ships which, with their poor windward ability, were forced right over to the Brazilian coast by the easterly winds just south of the equator. Indeed this is how Cabral stumbled on Brazil in 1500 on his voyage to India. So we too would sail down the western side of the South Atlantic, not far off the coast of Brazil, where wind and currents would be favourable to faster progress. After this the temptation is to take a short cut, as I had done when sailing around the world alone twenty-five years earlier. This had put me close to the centre of the high, which slowed me dramatically. I could have saved at least a week if I had continued due south directly into the Southern Ocean.

The Southern Ocean owes its richly deserved reputation as the world's roughest area to one simple accident of geography. It is the only stretch of water which completely circles the globe without interruption in the zone between the low pressure of Antarctica and the high pressure of the sub-tropics. In the southern hemisphere this means the prevailing wind is a westerly throughout the whole belt between Africa, Australia and South America to its north and Antarctica to its south. Since there are no land barriers to check its progress, this westerly wind blows uninterrupted around the world (which has a circumference of approximately 15,500 nautical miles at latitude 45°), and in doing so builds up a very large westerly sea and swell. This is why the region between 40°–50°S is called the roaring forties, and between 50°–60°S the screaming fifties. What drove most men there was the commercial advantages of a faster passage, made possible by the winds, although some went out of curiosity and in recent years yachtsmen have relished the challenge.

There is a theoretical limit to the size a wave can reach, supposedly 120 feet, and if this phenomenon occurs anywhere it will be in the Southern Ocean. The exceptional waves can be killers, especially when they break. On the great square-riggers they are known to have swept the decks of all obstructions, wheel, boats and deckhouses. They often caused broaches and knock downs which pushed them over on to their beam ends with a resultant cargo shift – a disaster from which few vessels recovered. Even the more modest size wave, such as a normal storm produces, can easily attain a height of sixty feet and be quite powerful enough casually to swamp, roll or capsize and obliterate any yacht. It was in these conditions that the square-riggers "ran their easting down", as they called sailing due east from roughly the small inhabited island of Tristan da Cunha, where they usually entered the Southern Ocean from the Atlantic. The crews on those ships, which were four times the length of *Enza*, reported being made to feel small by the waves.

Only at one point does the Southern Ocean meet any restrictions to its progress and this is where South America reaches southwards and Graham Land in Antarctica reaches northwards to narrow the gap from 2,000 miles to 600. This, too, is where the sea shallows, causing the waves to become shorter between crests and heap up. To pass through this gap, vessels must move to 56°S and round the formidable Cape Horn. Although the weather at the Horn can be as calm as the doldrums, the winds for the main part are westerly and accelerated by being forced down by the Andes into the gap known as Drake's Passage. It is for this reason that a westerly storm in the Southern Ocean is always more to be feared at the Horn than anywhere else.

Once clear of the Horn vessels used to take a wide sweep across the South Atlantic and take the more easterly side north to the equator which enabled them to enjoy the advantage of a south-easterly trade wind. After crossing the doldrums, there was a beat up through the north-east trade winds which were so favourable on the outward passage until, having passed through or around the Azores high pressure system, they met the south-westerlies of the North Atlantic which drove the vessels back to Europe. The total distance is some 27,250 nautical miles and to achieve this we needed an average speed of 14.2 knots or 16.3 land miles or 26 kilometres per hour.

Within three and a half hours we had our first crisis when the spinnaker halyard parted, depositing the sail into the sea. Our average speed had been 17.5 knots since the start and the wind had risen to 22 knots, a force 5 on the Beaufort Scale. Everything was going well until this happened. We recovered the sail with little damage, put Jaws aloft to reeve a new halyard and set the smaller spinnaker. The same pace was resumed but now we could not help worrying what had caused a halyard to break so soon. If breakages were to continue at this rate we would be unable to set spinnakers after a week and any hopes of beating even a hundred days would be slight. From this time onwards the spinnaker halyard was tightened or eased each hour to prevent one point becoming chafed through, in case that was the cause of the trouble.

We settled into a watch-keeping system of two on watch for three hours at a time: Jaws and I, Peter and Ed, David and Paul. George was out of it for the moment as he had been trying to get film back to the shore all morning. We had the first of the dried meals for supper, spaghetti bolognese and very good it was too, much better than anticipated. It was quickly established that Jaws was the king of spaghetti cooks. He had spent two years crewing a boat in Italy and learnt how to do it properly. Although the meals came in packets, each of the crew added his own flavouring contribution when it was his turn to cook, with everyone assuming, not always correctly, that my addition was lime pickle.

The wind rose to force 7 during the afternoon for a few hours, which enabled us to keep up the pressure, even with the increase in wave heights. *Enza* was easy to steer, despite the following seas, and occasionally we got a real swoop going and almost surfed along on the front of a wave. Those on watch had to keep alert though, as we sighted numerous baulks of timber any of which could have put a hole through the hulls. This became more worrying as darkness fell and it was no longer possible to observe the sea's surface properly despite the bright moonlight, but we had to put such thoughts out of our minds. Either we were racing or we weren't and if we were, then we had to press on. We crashed on through the night with fingers crossed and were rewarded by sighting Cape Villano lighthouse, just north of Cape Finisterre bearing east after just over twenty-two hours from Ushant. Our speed so far was 17.33 knots, nicely ahead of the average required for the voyage of 14.2 knots. But the wind was easing, just north of east to 9 knots at 0400. It was this light patch which worried Bob Rice when he advised us to go, but he had also said that it would only be temporary as a strong easterly would soon develop a little further south. He was proved right again as it lasted only four hours. Had we responded to the blandishments of the French and waited six hours to depart we would have been delayed far more, as *Commodore* was to discover.

One of the most impressive aspects of multihull sailing is the ability to sail faster than the wind in certain conditions. From passing Cape Finisterre until 2000 hours the same day the wind never rose above 14 knots, but during those sixteen hours we averaged just over 15 knots. We knew we must expect calmer conditions at stages during the course of the voyage, but if we could maintain speeds like this with comparatively little wind the chances of beating eighty days looked good. Morale rose accordingly. It received a greater boost as we rushed on through the night, the wind rising to 20 knots and then briefly to 32 knots the following day.

By 2000 hours on the 2nd February we had covered 424 miles in twenty-four hours. *Commodore* was 130 miles astern at noon when we spoke to them on the radio and exchanged positions, which was encouraging, although we were not sure whether to put this down to a superior performance on our boat's part or the delay caused by them missing the weather connection because they sailed six hours later. Of *Charal* there was little news except she was approaching the equator. It would have been nice to know what her lead amounted to, but de Kersuason was up to his usual tricks and refusing to say where he was. We supposed that by manufacturing a mystery, he imagined he was creating a news story, though we believed the true positions made for a much better tale. There had been talk of equipping all three boats with the Argos satellite tracking system before we sailed. This gives a position about every four hours and could have been made public, thus allowing everyone to see how we were all progressing. Unfortunately, it was never organised because the Jules Verne Association failed to raise enough money in time.

Our schedule called for us to pass the Canary Islands and transfer the first batch of film on the fifth day, but such was our speed we were there on the 3rd February, three and a half days into the voyage. This obliged the back-up team to charter a twin-engine aircraft and circle for an hour and a half whilst George transmitted all the film he had taken so far using the special microwave radio transmitter we carried for the purpose.

We probably lost ground keeping this rendezvous as we came in close to the Canary Islands to reduce their flying time and so fell foul of the wind shadows to leeward of all the islands. Luckily the wind did not ease much in strength but it swung into the north for a while, which forced us to sail more straight downwind to make the course we wanted. We played with various combinations of sail, trying to gain extra speed. Light wind is always harder work than strong wind as the sails need frequent adjustment and this requires greater concentration for frustratingly less reward.

Our speed dropped down to less than 12 knots, but *Commodore* was having similar difficulties and at midnight on the 4th they dropped back to a position 150 miles to the north-east. However, from now on tactics caused us to diverge. It had been our intention to cross the equator at about 26°W, about the middle of the old sailing ship track, but this involved what appeared to be an unprofitable gybe to the west, since the wind was back from the north-east. Our choice therefore was south or west and we chose to go south. *Commodore* planned to drop off the sixth member of the crew, a cameraman, as they sailed through the Cape Verde Islands. The poor man was due to be put in a rubber dinghy which they hoped would rendezvous with a powerboat, otherwise he would have some heavy paddling to do! To this end she gybed west, and far from being a disadvantage this turned out to be a huge bonus. By the 5th February, although the distance between us had increased, *Commodore* was already out to the west, where she found better winds. By midday on the 8th she had worked her way round us and was fourteen miles ahead. A day later when both boats crossed the equator, she extended this to sixty miles. We crossed at 21°W, and she at 26°W, where we had intended to be, and she got the better winds. Our time to the equator was 9 days, 6 hours and 33 minutes, *Commodore*'s around twelve hours faster and, as a result, she shattered every record in the book for a sailing vessel over this distance.

One of the great traditions amongst seagoers is the crossing the line ceremony. The degree of roughness involved in this initiation depends very much on the type of vessel. On liners passengers receive a light and decorous induction, whereas on a Merchant Navy cadet ship it was pretty rough and most people showed the marks for weeks afterwards whilst they regrew their hair! As a ceremony it was ancient 200 years ago in the time of Cook, and its origins are unknown, although it is not dissimilar to many customs undergone as young people are accepted into adulthood; the workplace rites on completing apprenticeship indentures being another example. It was always very much the crew's event, but could only happen with the compliance of the captain. Sometimes it involved a mild form of extortion, as officers could buy avoidance of the ceremony. But an unpopular officer might not be allowed this privilege as this was the one opportunity for the crew to get even for harsh or unfair treatment. A purser, for example, who was responsible for provisions, was always considered fair game since, whether the food was good or bad, the sailors always had a grouse about the quality and quantity served. It was a controlled form of anarchy because, whilst the ceremony was taking place, considerable authority devolved to the seaman playing the part of Neptune who would dictate the treatment to be meted out.

Aboard *Enza* there was only one candidate for the treatment, George Johns, since the rest of us had been inducted on earlier voyages and were already King Neptune's loyal subjects. Ed had been preparing for the ceremony for a while, noting down all the misdeeds to be included in the list of charges when the trial took place. From inside the godpod Peter and I would listen to Ed winding up George with threats of what was to come, to which George would respond by saying how much he was looking forward to it all. Come the great day we all spent considerable time preparing ourselves. Peter was Neptune, I was prosecutor, David was the defence, which did not involve much since his duties were to agree with the prosecution anyway. Paul and Jaws became the executioners while Ed, who was the chief instigator, elected to film the whole ceremony.

George was bundled away in the forward hull whilst we changed; Jaws looked particularly threatening. Then the victim was brought forward, told to kneel and we began to work our way through a dozen charges ranging from being Welsh to others that are best left unmentioned. As guilty was inevitably pronounced, part of the slops from the galley were thrown over the prisoner, whose clothes slowly tore or removed themselves. Filthy and eventually naked, George was finally accepted as a loyal subject by Neptune, free, in theory at least, from further goading by Ed. It provided an hour's amusement whilst the Autohelm steered and George could feel he has received a proper initiation, but he wisely confiscated the film!

Just south of the equator we were due to rendezvous with another plane to transmit more film and Steve Anscell, who was going to make a documentary about the voyage, flew out to Recife to charter an aircraft. We were still further east than intended and this put the only available aircraft on its limits as far as fuel was concerned. The pilot's proposals to carry spare fuel in jerrycans, which he had demonstrated whilst waving a lighted cigarette around, was not reassuring, and Steve sensibly cancelled the flight. Although equipped with a Garmin GPS he would still have had only twenty minutes over us, assuming he found us immediately, and this did not seem worth the dangers. Our next film-transmitting appointment was now south of Africa.

Meals continued to be produced by watches, so Jaws and I collaborated, as did Peter and Ed, known as father and son, and Paul and David. George got dragged into various teams when they thought he was becoming idle or at his request. These teams worked well, but Ed does get fixed ideas and when he and Peter were together, the decibel level from the galley usually rose. It culminated on the 10th February with a walk-out by Ed, who said the galley was not large enough for both of them, thereby confirming the old adage about two cooks in one kitchen. This disagreement, which had everyone else doubled up with laughter, was serious enough to last at least two minutes!

George's task inevitably made him the odd man out but at his own wish he became ever more involved in sailing the boat. He periodically joined watches and this had the benefit of widening the conversation, as after a couple of weeks people have usually talked each other out. They have learned all the family history, heard the funny stories, and the ship's gossip does not take long to discuss so, unless a thoughtful debate is instigated, having an additional person around brings welcome variety. I suppose because there was an enormous gap between George and the rest of us as far as experience was concerned, we found some of his questions odd. We were used to long periods at sea with its seclusion from the rest of the world, and no longer thought about the possible consequences of an accident or calamity which could be easily dealt with ashore, but represented considerable problems in our isolated little society. Thus a question such as "What happens if someone goes mad?" led to an unprintable reply from Paul, who, like the rest of us, had never considered the subject and therefore did not satisfy George's curiosity.

Commodore was still barrelling along about 200 miles to the west and ninety miles further south on the 10th, enjoying an easterly wind rather than our south-easterly, which meant the wind was freer and she could sail faster. As a result we were making averages of 360 miles a day but she was doing an extra twenty miles. We were not convinced she was a faster boat, our early progress showed the opposite might be true, especially when we were on a broad reach. But Peter and I had to accept she had obtained a more favourable slant to the wind by being west. To what extent this benefit was achieved because of their routier was hard to judge, but we had by this point decided to accept the French employment of a routier was not worth arguing about. We knew where the South Atlantic high was positioned from weatherfaxes and it seemed to be stalled at about 30°S and 30°W. We needed to sail round to the west of the high in order to keep the wind with us and the only way matters could improve was if the high moved east. To go straight through was asking to run into calms and even to go near the centre meant less wind. By the 12th February we were feeling the high's effects with lighter winds and calmer seas as we approached 18°S/28°W.

We passed the island of Trinidade, a lonely Brazilian sentinel out in the Atlantic, on the 13th February with the first sign of a small backing of the wind, but *Commodore* continued to extend her lead and was now able to turn eastwards and crossed to our south during the following night. This allowed us to close the gap slightly, as we were on the inside of the circle, and the lead narrowed to 134 miles as we both passed south of the high. On this day too, we learned de Kersuason was giving his position as 47°S/10°E, about 2,000 miles ahead. This was strange and suggested he had opened up on both of us since the equator, which seemed unlikely. Once again we regretted that Argos tracking was not fitted as, although we were swapping positions daily with *Commodore* and saw no reason why they should give incorrect information, we were not so trusting about those being credited to de Kersuason. Giving a false position used to be a great ploy, particularly by the French sailors twenty years ago, but over the years the drawbacks of doing this have been realised. Out on the oceans a fellow competitor is probably the nearest assistance if anything goes wrong and should disaster strike any search will logically start from the last reported position. If this is inaccurate then the chances of help or rescue are severely reduced.

This consideration was brought to our minds when we received a mild bump which none of us could explain shortly after passing the island. It was dark, nothing could be seen and a quick check of the boat showed all was well. A few days later though, when David was looking out through the galley window as the starboard hull rose a few feet from the sea, he noticed the bottom of the starboard dagger board was serrated. When the hull next emerged he confirmed that we had lost the bottom tip of the board. Goodness knows what caused it, but it must have been a powerful blow as the boards were very strong. He waited for the next lift to check the rudder was all right, since rudders are vulnerable to anything passing beneath a boat. Fortunately, there was no sign of damage. In fact from now on until we re-entered the northern hemisphere and came on the wind again, the boards were irrelevent, as we anticipated sailing off the wind for most of the time, but their presence, protruding three to seven feet below the boat, meant they would, we hoped, absorb the shock of striking objects instead of the less robust and absolutely essential rudders. Since both the French boats were constantly reporting assorted damage we decided to keep this news to ourselves. It was not too serious and we were reluctant to join a competition of dreaming up dramas in order to make headlines.

On the 14th February, we were 25° S and the wind was from east by south. By the 15th we had reached 32°S, it was backing east and during the day it continued to back round almost to the north. On the 16th the wind backed again until it steadied from the west, the first noticeable influence of the Southern Ocean winds and, as if to confirm this, a giant wandering albatross, with a wing span of more than eleven feet, cruised past in its eternal search for food.

It is an axiom that if a boat wants to head east from anywhere in the South Atlantic, such as Punta del Este in the Whitbread Race or Cape Town in the BOC, then the secret is to head hard south until well into the westerlies which are usually found at about 40°S. Cutting the corner by sailing south-east may seem smarter but this usually ensures that the boat is in lighter winds far longer, whereas those who have headed due south pick up the stronger winds and gain as a result. The benefit of these tactics were now being demonstrated as *Commodore*, being further south and nearer to the westerly wind belt, opened the lead to 250 miles. We were still in lighter winds and could do nothing but follow, knowing that soon we would be in the same pattern and then, we hoped, begin to narrow the gap. Our turn came on the 17th February when the westerly wind rose to a half gale.

The evening sky on the 16th as we sailed south-eastwards through 37°S at 17 knots was impressive. A bright yellow horizon deepened to orange and then slowly to mauve and finally blue. What, we wondered, did this portend? By midnight the wind had risen only 5 knots, to 19 knots, but our average speed was an impressive 22 knots. Paul was steering as we saw and quickly passed a fishing boat which must have wondered what on earth was happening as we surged round it doing a fantastic surf of 28.4 knots which woke everyone. Shortly afterwards David also hit 28 knots. The scene was wonderful. Astern were two faint rocket trails caused by the bioluminescence disturbed in the wake but otherwise all around was pitch black, the only illumination coming from the compass and instrument lights which showed the cold spray and water whipping across the cockpit. By 0500 the wind veered to the north-west and reached 28 knots, so we gybed, handed the genoa and set the small spinnaker. It was crazy and exhilarating sailing but, finding life a little too exciting as the seas rose, we took one reef in the main to make steering easier.

Wind pressure on the sails varies with the wind's strength, the amount of sail set and the aspect of the sails to the wind. Boats seem over-pressed when they have too much sail set or soggy when they are carrying too little. The boat tells you this by her feel, by the way she responds to the helm and to the waves. When she is slow and sluggish she probably wants more sail, when bouncing sharply she is usually all right and when she feels under pressure she could do with a little less. All boats vary, even sister yachts will not respond identically if they are loaded differently, and it is the skill of the helmsman or skipper which will decide when sails need to be changed or adjusted. Mistakes can lose time or lead to mast or gear failures. This is not a skill to be learned from books, it is instinctive and acquired by experience. These days, when boats are lighter and sailed faster than formerly, this instinct for the correct balance is even more important. I like to get my legs well spread when on the helm in hairy conditions, as my feet act as sensors for the amount of heel and, of course, it keeps me more stable. But when you have the confidence there is nothing like steering a boat at full pelt. The speed is thrilling, reactions have to be fast and that little extra concentration which leads to gaining an extra yard or two from each wave brings great rewards.

Our average speed fell slightly, to 20 knots, as the rising seas forced us to take things a little more carefully. We were surging forward on the larger waves which put too much strain on the gear and memories of an experimental carbon fibre mast which failed on *Condor* in 1977 were always at the back of my mind, although technology had moved on a great deal since then. Nevertheless, I still do not know how you tell when a carbon fibre mast is at its limits. It is a little more obvious with wood or aluminium.

Although we had not yet crossed the 40th parallel of latitude this was roaring forties sailing and the ease with which the boat handled was immensely cheering, although for safety we decreed a max-imum speed of 25 knots. If we went consistently above that, it was time for reductions in sail, as we had to remember there were another sixty-two days to go, or, as we were now three days ahead of schedule, perhaps only fifty-nine, and it was pointless to risk breakages.

If we needed any confirmation that this policy was right, we received a message from London that morning saying *Charal* reported striking ice with the starboard float which had removed the forward part. She was now easing her way slowly northwards with the intention of heading to Cape Town for repairs. Olivier de Kersuason was effectively out of the race. Confusion was caused as the position *Charal* gave was no further on than the one she reported two days previously and later she announced yet another one, this time in longitude 3°E, or 7°W of the earlier position. If we were to take this literally it would mean *Charal* had been moving backwards for two days! Despite de Kersuason's determinedly maverick stance, we had to sympathise with the man and his crew who must all have been devastated by the accident and we were relieved they had survived it. Their performance had not been as good as *Commodore*'s or ours; in fact when she pulled out *Charal* was only 1,200 miles ahead, when she should have been 2,000 miles for an eighty-day circumnavigation. Nevertheless we had lost a hare of sorts and the Southern Ocean would be that bit more lonely as a result.

Originally when we discussed our sailing plan, we agreed it would be advisable to stick close to the 40th parallel and only dip further southwards as we approached Australia, unless the high centre moved south, in which case we would follow it to retain the wind strength. Normally to choose a route further south means sailing closer to the centres of the low pressure systems which give stronger winds and larger seas. We estimated that 20–25 knots of wind from the south-west was adequate to hold the required average of 17 knots through the Southern Ocean, and there was no point in looking for more. Now, after *Charal*, we had the threat of ice to consider.

Despite the excellent progress and a day's run of nearly 400 miles, *Commodore*, who was almost 4° to the south, was still opening up the lead, albeit slowly. When we exchanged messages that evening she was 286 miles ahead and enjoying similar weather, although we thought her seas might be slightly larger, which should inhibit her speed, since they were closer to the centre of the low pressure system and the isobars closer together. Indeed this proved to be the case as over the next fifteen hours we maintained the same speed whilst they sailed a knot slower.

It was far from easy, though. Conditions aboard *Enza* were wet and cooking was difficult. In the godpod Peter and I were thrown about and when large waves smashed into its bottom we were tossed upwards from our bunks, in extreme cases hitting the deckhead above. Crossing from hull to pod or back was dangerous. If a wave swept over the boat, a not uncommon occurrence, its force picked a person up like a tennis ball and carried him along until the wave subsided, leaving a gasping and soaked crewman grounded on the netting. It happened to all of us and it was often necessary to turn off down wind to reduce the risks when someone wanted to cross from one hull to the other. All in all, however, we were quite snug, with sufficient food and rest, although the quantity of sleep depended on the antics of the boat.

Aboard *Commodore* the situation must have been far worse and the exposed steering positions in the hulls definitely adding to the stresses of the job. They had the same problem with crossing the trampoline from hull to hull and no protection halfway as we had with our godpod. It transpired they also turned off down wind when anyone wanted to transfer from side to side, an action they referred to as 'calling for a taxi'. Some people pretend to enjoy being uncomfortable, thinking it macho, but an uncomfortable person cannot concentrate well, and cold, wet clothing inhibits performance. The fact that *Commodore* was further south therefore seemed to be advantageous for us at the moment, though it gave her a slightly shorter distance to sail. Nevertheless we were well aware that we might be forced to join her if the winds eased.

That same day, during a routine structure inspection, David came up with a worrying report. The starboard dagger board case was bulging under the pressure of the water created by the speed and leaking into the hull. This was not a structural problem and we could have simply sealed off the relevant compartment and left the water to slosh around. It would add a little weight, but it was hardly crucial at this stage. David, however, believed he could effect repairs using underwater epoxy plus any available bits and pieces. The plan was to beef up the walls of the casing to stop it flexing and then attempt to plug the leak, but the weather was far from ideal for this sort of work. For a start, just getting across the boat and down through the forward hatch was asking for a dowsing and, even if we turned off downwind and wave when they wanted to get below, we could not see them to do the same for their return journey. Conditions below were very cramped. There was a small manhole but you had to go on hands and knees to enter it and then squirm round past the casing once half through the hole. The light was provided by an electric torch and there were complications with jamming it into a position so it would give steady illumination where needed and not be shaken around. Finally there was the crazy motion of the boat, the sudden pounding against waves and the little fountain of water when the boat accelerated. Small wonder

David took to referring to the casing compartments as the dungeons!

We slowed a little. This was essential as otherwise the epoxy would never have stayed in place whilst it hardened. We should ideally have slowed more but, as it was, the reduction in speed cost us sixty miles over the day and none of us, not even the workers, could stand the thought of losing more. This leak continued to give trouble but at least the repair reduced it to a trickle. A precautionary check of the port casing showed it to be in a similar state, so the gang treated that as well. David and his assistants were spending more time on boat-building at this stage than they were sailing. It was very aggravating as the problem should have shown up on the Atlantic delivery trip but either it was not so bad then, or we had been unobservant.

On the 19th February we recorded a 340-mile day and *Commodore* was 270 miles ahead. Twenty-four hours later, after we covered 357 miles, this lead was reduced to 200 miles. Strong winds had once more built up huge seas and 'Les Boys', as the French press called the *Commodore* crew, frightened themselves by running down the front of a particularly nasty wave which threatened to roll them. The big Southern Ocean greybeard was everyone's ultimate fear and we wondered how large this French example had been. The incident certainly seemed to confirm that the policy of keeping out of the path of depressions was the right one. Morale rose but was promptly dampened by the large spinnaker tearing and falling into the sea. We recovered the pieces with some difficulty as, even under mainsail alone, speeds were in excess of 17 knots. At one stage Paul and I had the only grip on one corner and could see the extent of the damage. We looked at each other both thinking the same thing – repairs would take ages and it was extremely doubtful whether we could make a sufficiently good job to rely upon this particular sail again. Maybe it would save everyone time and effort if we just let go and gave the sail to Davy Jones. Then we started to haul in like fishermen with their nets since you never know. Everything else might be a write-off before long and even a roughly repaired sail would be better than nothing.

Modern communications can give a false sense of security aboard a boat in these latitudes. The instant contact now available tends to remove the feeling of isolation from the rest of mankind that was an inevitable part of sailing here twenty-five years ago. In some ways this is a loss as it also detracts from the true feeling of adventure which comes from being totally dependent upon one's own devices. Nevertheless the damage to *Charal*, and *Commodore*'s near miss brought home to everyone just how far removed we really were from assistance and the loneliness of the area we were now traversing. It is one of the least densely populated areas on the planet, visited occasionally by ships and, of course, yachts in the regular calendar of races around the world. In fact this isolation was about to be rudely shattered by the ten yachts in the British Steel Challenge fleet who had just left Hobart in Tasmania bound for Cape Town. We made contact on the Satcom and set up a radio schedule. On our first radio chat they advised us to be careful of the wall of steel heading in our direction. The answer we gave was that in a hurricane a wisp of straw can be driven straight through an oak! They were beating to the west, we were fast reaching to the east and at some point we would rush past each other at a closing speed of perhaps 25 knots. We were unlikely to see any of them in practice, but it was worth keeping in touch just to ensure we did not make fools of ourselves by an accidental collision.

By the 21st we were 530 miles from Cape Town and the gap with *Commodore* had narrowed further to 180 miles. We received visual confirmation of this when Steve Anscell flew over in a C-130 Hercules aircraft of 27 Squadron of the South African Air Force. It circled for nearly two hours whilst we transmitted film to them by the same means as before. When all George's film was despatched and we'd managed some interviews, we were treated to a dramatic low-level fly past before the aircraft soared away to film *Commodore*. They had been looking for *Charal* but with no success, hardly surprising in view of the vague and varied positions she was giving.

Two hundred miles may not seem much, but it can be sufficient to ensure very different weather conditions. Watching the whorls and spirals on the weather map sent over the fax machine, we could see quieter weather approaching from the west where the isobars were edging apart, which would mean less speed for us. Although at the moment we were coping well and sailing fast with winds up to 32 knots, we decided to chance it and head south in order to keep the isobars at the same distance apart, which should enable us to maintain current wind strength. In the next two days we travelled five degrees south, whilst *Commodore* moved down only two. Inevitably, we anticipated losing some ground to them by taking a slightly more divergent course from the rhumb line (the direct distance to our next mark south of Tasmania), but we expected to gain slightly from being closer to the pole where fewer miles are required to cover each degree of longitude. For the mathematically inclined, the number of miles per degree of longitude is equal to 60 miles × cosine latitude. Thus at 60°S only thirty miles are needed to cross a degree of longitude as opposed to 60 miles at the equator.

In fact we were horrified at the amount of distance we lost. We had enjoyed 22 knots of wind whilst the Hercules was with us and this rose to 32 knots overnight, which did not stop us holding on to the full mainsail. We thought we were sailing really fast until we received *Commodore*'s position on the 22nd February and discovered she was now 263 miles ahead, a gain of eighty-three miles in twenty-four hours, or an average of 3.5 knots. As we averaged over 14 knots this meant that she achieved 18 knots, a very impressive performance. The situation was even worse on the 23rd when she was 357 miles ahead. Admittedly, the wind had fallen to 10 knots as the calmer conditions overhauled us first, whilst they still enjoyed much stronger winds. But we now had to face the possibility of their being in a different weather system, which meant that luck with the weather would have a far greater influence on relative progress in future. The quiet belief that we had the faster boat and could beat them eventually was beginning to be rocked as we failed to close up. We needed to take back the initiative urgently.

Spurred, and with a rising wind as we finally profited from moving south, we pumped up the weather ballast tank. The logbook shows the number of speeding tickets issued in the next twenty-four hours whenever the log exceeded the new limit of 27 knots. (This had crept up from the original 25 knots.) Some were for speeds in excess of 30 knots. Despite having to ease up for a while to allow more repairs to the port dagger board casing, the result was the best day's run to date of 476.5 miles, almost 20 knots. It was exciting, tense and noisy sailing but this was more like it and we waited impatiently to see how well

Commodore had fared. When we received her position we could hardly believe it, we had taken an incredible 200 miles out of her in twenty-four hours. In other words we averaged 8 knots faster all day. The light weather we had suffered had now caught up with them, whilst we were just ahead of the next depression. The gap between the two boats was suddenly down to 157 miles, we could almost see their wake ahead and our spirits rose accordingly.

When travelling at high speeds, the disproportionate loss of distance when forced to slow down for any reason was emphasised when Peter and Ed gybed without reefing the mainsail first. This was our normal practice as, if the full main was gybed, the full width battens which held the sail stiff whipped across and could easily be snapped. Peter was for reefing, Ed said don't bother, but after some discussion they gybed without reefing and every single batten broke from top to bottom. The crack woke most of us and those who slumbered through were rudely awakened by Peter's affronted yell at Ed. "Don't persuade me to do things against my better judgement in future!"

It took all hands nearly eight hours to replace the battens from the store of spares we carried. They are not easy to fit and we had to unbolt each from its mast track, work out the broken one and then insert the new. The boat did not stop, of course, as the headsail was set, but the repair probably cost about forty miles. It also left us with insufficient battens for another complete replacement, so the rule that we take at least two reefs before gybing was re-emphasised. Meanwhile *Commodore*, now in the stronger winds which had overtaken us, inevitably edged ahead because of this delay but only by twenty miles. In view of the time lost through our own stupidity, we were lucky it was not a great deal more.

Geographically we were now a short distance to the north of Marion Island, a small South African meteorological outpost. On the weatherfax we could see a complicated double depression slowly moving south into the Southern Ocean from Madagascar and the projections showed that *Commodore* ought to get trapped between the two centres, an area that would have little wind. It looked as if we might just have an opportunity to overtake them at last, but only if we changed course to go south of the same system. Unfortunately, once on this course, although the wind remained in the 26–30-knot span, speed had to be reduced as we brought the south-westerly seas round on to the beam and there was still a residual southerly swell.

There is nothing more difficult to cope with at sea than two wave formations coming from different directions. If you set the boat up to be right for one, you can be sure the other will cause trouble. In this case the waves from the south made the boat pound or slam into the other waves and we received constant heavy thumps beneath the godpod which made sleep impossible. Eventually we were forced to ease back towards the original course, closer to east, in order to reduce the punishment *Enza* was taking. The boat was designed for high-speed motorways not farm tracks and, if we pressed on, we would undoubtedly regret it. When I spoke to Cam Lewis, an American member of the *Commodore* crew, on the 25th February I told him we were easing up whilst the conditions were so uncooperative. There seemed to be audible relief in his voice as he acknowledged that they were also finding things pretty miserable and indeed the day's runs showed they had also slowed and only made an extra six miles on us in very similar weather. Cam and I often exchanged news, sometimes on the fax, sometimes by voice. He specialised in lovely winding-up sentences at the end of his messages such as, "Shred the planet." Another time he quoted the price of dry socks aboard *Commodore*. It helped to visualise the domestic scene and each time I felt more thankful than ever that we had the godpod.

For both boats to have similar weather was a rare occurrence and the next day we reverted to having different winds, which allowed them to stretch the lead by a hundred miles, although they paid the price as they reported more damage. Watching the weatherfaxes, however, we could see the calm patch approaching and that they were making no attempt to avoid it. We held our breath and hoped they would continue to miss the warning signs.

All the time we had been concentrating on *Commodore* the miles were whistling past. In the ten days since we first picked up the Southern Ocean winds we covered 3,704 miles and maintained an average speed of 15.44 knots. We were running three days ahead of the schedule for an eighty-day circumnavigation and hopes were high. We had suffered no serious damage, our faith in the boat was total and we believed we could beat *Commodore*. In fact we were becoming convinced by the quantity of breakages they were reporting and their general attitude that it was unlikely they would get past Australia. So it was essential to keep applying the pressure by holding the present speed and making equal runs, as this seemed enough to make them nervous and take risks. They had been lucky in that the slow accumulation of breakages they declared had yet to handicap them seriously, but how long could this last? As it turned out it was Bruno and his crew who were sailing under a benevolent star, their luck held, ours failed.

On the 26th February we passed about 160 miles north of the Crozet Islands in 50°E longitude. The seas were still confused and we were bashing along beneath a lowering dark sky. David and Paul were making the most of the tricky conditions an hour before midnight when Jaws suddenly put his head out from the starboard hatch and yelled that the accommodation area was flooded. We struggled out of sleeping bags as David confirmed Jaws's report. All hands and get busy with buckets was the order whilst a search was made for the source. The most obvious place was the dagger board case but this was no worse than usual. Next we examined the aft compartment where the generator was housed and this was half full as well. Another area to be baled. It was a surreal situation – Paul calmly at the helm with George dutifully filming in floodlights and filming lights which lit up an area of frantic activity in what was otherwise a pitch-black and windswept night.

The generator compartment quickly responded to baling and was soon dry again. This was puzzling, as there were plenty of connections to the sea in this area, a likely source of the trouble, but all these were fine. In the accommodation area the WC had sea cocks and these were closed but, although the water level hardly fell, we could find no obvious hole. It was almost an hour before the explanation was discovered and the reason it took so long was that the balers were standing on it – a large L-shaped gash in the hull running about one foot parallel to the keel and then rising in a curve away towards the water-line. The crack went right through the hull and exposed the core of the structure.

Peter, David and I withdrew to the cockpit for a chat. We carried underwater slow-hardening epoxy on board but this was a major tear which could not realistically be sealed on the outside whilst the boat was afloat. If it was left untouched, the rush of water past was bound to work away at it and the crack would quickly become a hole. We could block off the accommodation area and limit the extent of flooding but how long could we continue to race before the whole hull started to split apart? We could go to the French-owned Kerguelen Islands, not far away now, where there was a small settlement and some facilities. Even if we got there in one piece, however, we would need help and materials to carry out an effective repair and that involved employing outside assistance, which was against the Jules Verne rules.

Knowing the temptation is to take the least energetic choice when things look hopeless and you are tired, we went through the alternatives again. But it did not matter which way we looked at the situation, there was only one choice and that was to head for the nearest port at a speed the hulls could take. As far as the Jules Verne Trophy was concerned, we were out of it and *Commodore* had the race to herself.

4

The End of the Dream

Jaws explained what had happened. He was fast asleep and was suddenly awakened by a bang. Since few people sleep as heavily as Jaws, the fact that he heard it at all meant it was extremely loud, although not sufficient to rise above the background noise of the boat crashing along and carry to the crew on watch in the cockpit. He thought it was about ten minutes later that he sensed something was wrong and woke properly. He heard the sound of sloshing water, jumped out of his bunk, and found himself thigh deep in cold Southern Ocean – we knew the rest.

It was 0200 on the 27th. We had taken down the mainsail and were sailing gently northwards under staysail. The ballast pump was set up to pump out the starboard accommodation area and, provided it was switched on for ten in every twenty minutes, the water-level was kept under control. We reduced the watches to one person on duty. There was little need of a large crew on deck in these circumstances and it was better to let everyone have a rest and recover from the shock because, once daylight came, there would be work to do. The good news was that we were not in danger. At worst one compartment might flood, in which case we'd lose the WC and the three bunks in the starboard hull, but the boat would still float and it was simple to prevent water flooding neighbouring compartments. The major risk was from the crack opening further or the hull core material delaminating as the water soaked it, but the honeycomb texture meant only the exposed surface would soften, so it would take time for a large area to become affected.

We had telexed *Commodore* the moment we realised we were out of the race and wished them every success. Their feelings can be imagined. Suddenly the pressure was off and they could ease up a little and stop taking so many risks. All they had to do now was beat the clock, but that remained a very elusive target and our competition had been providing them with a stimulus. Within two days they also reported a crack in the hull which they slowed to repair and then ran straight into the calm gap between the two low pressure centres, as we had foreseen. This lost them more time and it was galling to think that, had we not been disabled, we would probably have caught up and even gone ahead.

However, our immediate priority now was to get north out of the Southern Ocean into an area of smaller waves where the chances of the crack widening as the hull flexed were lessened. Then we had to decide whether to go east or west to reach land. The distance to South Africa was shorter but if we headed there we would have to cross the South Indian Ocean high pressure area to obtain the necessary easterly winds. Australia was further away but downwind and therefore it was probably quicker to sail to Fremantle, but this took us further from base in England. We weighed the alternatives and opted to head for Cape Town, as we knew we could haul out there and the trip from Cape Town to Southampton was a reasonable one.

The southerly winds, which had given us such a rough time whilst we were sailing eastwards, now proved useful and pushed us slowly north before beginning to ease. The sea temperature rose to 15°C, so David went overside with a mask to examine the damage. The outer crack pattern was similar to that inside and he could see torn carbon fibre reinforcing close to the keel where it formed a strong backbone. There was no immediate danger but his inspection confirmed the boat should not be pressed in her present state and we should abandon all hopes of racing, advice echoed by Nigel Irens when we spoke over the radio. I suppose it made us feel slightly better to know all the experts agreed that the boat should be repaired properly as soon as possible, but it was still hard to accept that we were out of the race.

The South Indian Ocean high pressure system was moving south-wards behind the two depressions and for the next five days the wind never rose above 10 knots. Watching the clouds for the easterly winds, we could see a huge circle of cloud which we assumed marked the centre of the system but it stubbornly stuck where it was for three days as we drifted slowly north at between 4–5 knots. When speed dropped to a knot we all went swimming, which allowed everyone an opportunity to inspect the hull and admire the break at the bottom of the dagger board. George decided to film the damage and went overside armed with one of his video cameras. Later he discovered that the watertight housing should have been designated showerproof as seawater had got into the casing and wetted the camera. This jammed the tape release mechanism so he attacked it with a screwdriver.

"What are you doing, George?"

"I'm just removing a couple of screws so that I can take the tape out."

An hour later one fine piece of craftsmanship had been reduced to 700 pieces of metal, silicon chips and lenses. He removed the tape all right, but the camera was wrecked. George's reputation as a precision engineer, never strong, took a severe dent!

With the sea-water temperature now up to 21°, swimming was a pleasant relaxation as we wandered very slowly through the high pressure system. Our get up and go had got up and gone, we were cruising without motivation. A lethal card school developed, the stake being jugs of rum and coke to be settled on arrival in Cape Town. Ed, a bookmaker's delight, showed a masochistic tendency to try and improve his luck and went steadily deeper into debt. We were still heading for Cape Town but a forecast of 25-knot south-westerly winds made us rethink. The boat was in no fit state to bash into any sort of weather, especially this close to where the Agulhas Current sweeps down from the Indian Ocean at up to 5 knots and in storms can create wicked square-shaped giant waves which have broken supertankers in half. Consequently we headed for East London to shelter until the weather brightened and arrived there during the morning of the 9th March. Paul lost the card game to decide who was to act as ship-keeper and everyone else went ashore for a proper meal. When we returned, a nervous Paul was prowling the deck armed with a stick. A puff adder had been driven into the water alongside and he was not sure whether it had climbed on board. We had an uneasy night!

We sailed the next morning, picking up a strong north-easter which pushed us easily round the bottom of Africa towards the Cape of Good Hope. Progress was good for a day and then the wind turned south-westerly again and we dived for the nearest shelter at Mossel Bay, a small port which was the scene of the first European landing by Bartholomew Dias in 1488. This time we had to wait two days for the wind to turn favourable and even then it went back to the south-west before we reached Cape Agulhas, the southermost point of Africa. From there on we had to tack to the Cape of Good Hope, keeping relatively close to the shore past such notorious landmarks as Danger Point, the scene of the *Birkenhead* disaster a century ago which established the principle of women and children first into the life-boats. We eventually moored up in Cape Town late on the 14th March. It had taken sixteen days to cover 2,000 miles from the position of the accident.

Cape Town was my first real foreign port when I went to sea as an apprentice in 1957 and it is still one of my favourites. Its setting, sheltered by the 3,500-foot-high Table Mountain, one of the world's most familiar landmarks, is unbeatable. The mountain, or at least the cloud above it, can be seen thirty-five miles out at sea and has been a welcome landfall for sailors for five centuries. It has one of the most pleasant climates I know, which used to make it an attraction for captains with sick crews but also earned it the nickname of 'the Tavern of the Seas' in the days before the Suez Canal. The port continues to attract a wide variety of shipping and it could provide the full repair facilities we required.

We were met on arrival by Brian Aitken and a party from Enza. No one could say what the future held as everything would depend upon the Board's attitude. At present the whole thing looked like a disaster, but we were not so convinced and certainly did not feel like a disaster. Until the accident we had averaged 347 miles per day or 14.47 knots. The target was 14.2 knots and we were pushing up the average slightly every day to build a nice cushion against any calms we might have met on the homeward run through the Atlantic. We believed we had done enough to show the eighty-day target was beatable. At this stage, too, *Commodore* was not making particularly fast progress and there was a good chance she would fail. As a crew we got on well and made a good team, we wanted another stab at what we regarded as unfinished business. Brian was supportive but neutral to start with, then the TV and press coverage reports began to arrive. Eighty-four TV stations in fifty-seven countries had been taking the film we sent back, demonstrating the demand for this sort of adventure and the objective of publicising the name Enza was more than achieved. The Board might still be hesitating but Brian could see just how effective the whole campaign had been and flew back to New Zealand with a mission.

Before Brian left we had to settle the bet about my smoking. Had I won or not? The original deal had stated I must give up for the voyage. Well, the voyage was over, but in a shorter time and not the way we anticipated. Brian decided that I *had* won, but under what he called Kiwi Rules the champagne prize had to be shared among all the crew, which was fair, since they claimed to have done the suffering whilst I had withdrawal symptoms. If they did, it was in a good cause.

When we set out in January I was so confident that the voyage would be completed non-stop that I left my passport at home. This presented no problems with South African immigration, nor did I have any difficulties when I went to a department store to buy clothes and used my credit card, which I was carrying as it would not be damaged by water. However, when I went to a bank to obtain cash, a sum less than I had just spent on clothing, I was refused. I was told my credit card was no use without some other form of identification. I tried three different banks without success but at the fourth they asked if anyone in Cape Town could identify me, a picture in the previous day's newspapers being considered insufficient. Baffled, I suggested they phone the Royal Cape Yacht Club Secretary, who listened to my voice and was able to say I was who I claimed to be and, hey presto, I had money. Naturally I was delighted but left somewhat puzzled by the bank's security system!

A year short of the first multi-racial elections there was only a slight tension in Cape Town. Whilst some forecast doom, more saw the demise of white rule as inevitable and welcomed the opportunities which would occur when international trade sanctions were lifted.

We made arrangements to haul *Enza* out of the water. The Capetonians could be forgiven if they were slightly blasé about very large multihulls by this time, as *Charal* had sailed for France just two days before we arrived, having completed sufficient repairs to get home. This was our plan, too, and we thought we would have a shot at the Cape Town – Southampton record on the way. But first we had to remove the effects of a heavy overnight oil spill which had completely covered the waterline in the main basin. It was filthy and we were furious. The press could hardly miss our anger and criticism which duly appeared in the newspapers the next day. This led to a large man coming round from the Port Authority saying they were not very pleased with our comments. *He* was not pleased!

Once Cape Town's huge floating crane had lifted Enza clear of the water and the size of the hole was visible, it was quite alarming. The starboard dagger board looked terrible with its jagged lower end. David started at once ripping out the core to get back to dry cells to assess the damage fully, whilst we brought in a local boatbuilder who was experienced with the materials. The actual cause of our accident was never satisfactorily established, but even before we arrived in South Africa some of the press had decided we had hit a submerged container and once that story was printed it was very hard to persuade anyone that the answer might be different. If it was a submerged container it was unique as it defied all Archimedes' principles. As any submariner will tell you, it is almost impossible to obtain an equilibrium between weight and buoyancy and hold a stable depth without moving. It is the hydroplanes that hold the submarine level and they only work when water is passing them. In any case the hole did not look in the least as if it was made by a sharp object like the corner of a container. A tree or log was possible, but only if the boat had smashed down on to its end rather heavily. More likely was a whale, although there was no positive evidence to support this and fatigue or stress could not be ruled out either. The boat was not new and maybe we had applied too much pressure to the hull in our efforts to keep pushing in rough conditions. If the record were to be attempted again, it would help to know the cause, so that we could make the necessary improvements.

The boat was going to be returned to England for full repairs and she would be carried aboard a reefer ship courtesy of Enza's South African rivals, the Cape Fruit Marketing Board. We prepared her for

The beginning of it all. Above, in America the crane is set up to lift *Tag* into the water. Below, stepping *Enza*'s carbon fibre mast at its interesting rake.

Above, *Enza* emerging from the shed at Hamble after her first refit, and below, moored astern of *Commodore* in Brest harbour before the first attempt.

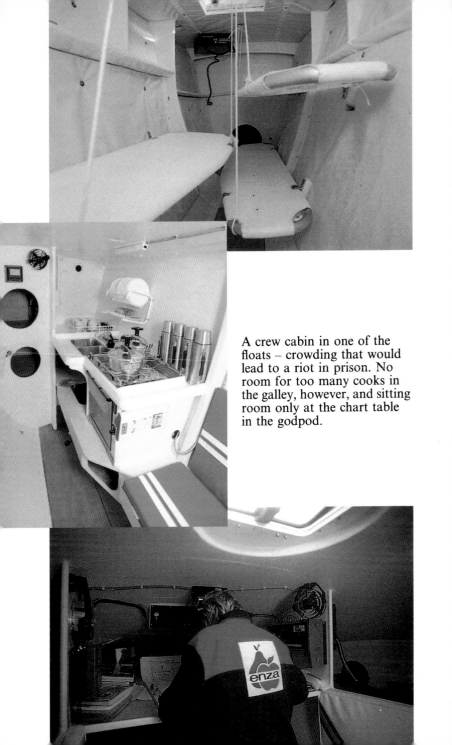

A crew cabin in one of the floats – crowding that would lead to a riot in prison. No room for too many cooks in the galley, however, and sitting room only at the chart table in the godpod.

Enza at speed with fully reefed mainsail on the first attempt.

Above, craning out at Cape Town after abandoning the first attempt, and below the reason why. Although the dagger board damage would not have stopped us, the hole in the hull would.

Above left, Cam Lewis, Peter, Robin and Bruno Peyron at *Commodore*'s triumphant return. Above right, the one and only Olivier de Kersuason. Below, the team for the second attempt, left to right: Peter, Robin, David, Angus, Ed, George, Barry, Jaws.

Above, *Enza* showed a noticeable increase in pace after the second refit. Below, *Enza* leads *Lyonnaise* out from Brest harbour at the start of the second attempt.

Above left, if we weren't steering we were working around the deck, in this case scraping burrs off the mainsheet track, and right, repacking the spinnaker. But crossing the line gave an excuse for relaxation as Angus is initiated into Neptune's kingdom.

shipping, put the mast on chocks, removed the rudders and lowered the radio and wind generator masts. Jaws was to travel on the ship whilst the rest of us went our various ways. Peter had already left to talk to our sponsors in New Zealand. David and I arranged to fly to London. There was a small drama on the evening we were due to fly as we went to the boat for a last check and discovered the door into the nacelle had been forced. The same thing had happened the previous day and some of our clothing was stolen, so I jumped into the cockpit and peered round the corner. It was a shock to come face to face with the thief, sitting at the chart table bold as brass. The threat of a boot in the face kept him sitting where he was until the police arrived, but I wasn't going to miss my plane by staying behind to press charges. So presumably somewhere in Crossroads Township someone is learning that clothing designed for the polar regions is not ideal in the South African climate and goodness knows what he has done with my Henri Lloyd air-filled survival suit!

5

Unfinished Business

Enza returned to Sheerness in May and we took the MFV *Morayshire* down river from St Katharine's Dock to collect her. We arrived just ahead of the reefer ship with her distinctive red and white cargo lying across No. 1 hatch. It did not take long to lower the cat into the water, place the mast across the deck and get underway. Those of us who had travelled down on the *Morayshire* were recovering from experiments to create a Docklands spaghetti sauce, called Wappingnaise. The secret was to have two cooks with backs to each other so neither could see what the other was doing and then combine the result. It tasted far nicer than might be expected, although a mysterious curry influence was very noticeable. We towed back up river and discovered that, without the rudders or keels installed, *Enza* swung all over the place, despite all our efforts involving crossing the towing lines, which were also lengthened and shortened but to no avail. She just wanted to yaw. We moored up on the buoys outside the lock gate. It would have been preferable to go into the dock, but *Enza* is 42 feet wide and the lock will only accommodate 32 feet of beam. Safely secured, she remained there whilst her future was decided.

The real problem was one of PR. The original objective was to beat eighty days and in this we had failed. This failure would be unimportant if Bruno had been unsuccessful as well, but after trailing the average required all the way through the Southern Ocean and back north through the Atlantic, he suddenly ran into favourable winds right at the very end and stormed home in 79 days, 6 hours, 15 minutes and 56 seconds to become the deserving first winner of the Jules Verne

Trophy. It was a brilliant performance by all five crewmen and a record for the history books, but sadly the Association failed to raise the million dollars' prize money.

If we were to be given another chance we would have to beat Bruno's record. But at least we now knew it was possible. Peter and I went over to La Baule to see *Commodore* return to a deserved hero's reception but it was hard not to grit one's teeth when congratulating the crew. The motivation was sufficient for us, but could it justify a PR return to a sponsor?

Fortunately, Brian Aitken believed there was mileage in another attempt and was in New Zealand putting forward strong arguments to the Apple and Pear Marketing Board. Bruno's win was not exactly helpful, but a world record is a world record, especially if promoted properly, and the additional costs of another attempt would be relatively small as we had the boat, the crew and the potential. When asked what we considered might be a sensible target we quoted seventy-seven days, an average of more than 14.74 knots. One or two people sucked their teeth but we were not in the habit of giving unrealistic figures.

What swung matters our way was a large New Zealand apple harvest and low international prices for fruit which increased the need for advertising, the excellent TV coverage figures, and finally a challenge from Titouan Lamazou. He was still struggling to have his boat repaired, but the sponsor wanted him to go for the record as soon as he was ready. They had spent far more money than Enza and the boat had achieved nothing, they urgently needed an event to gain publicity for their investment. A race between a huge monohull and a huge multihull would be a great story, certainly more exciting than a race against the clock on its own, especially since many traditional yachtsmen remained unconvinced that multihulls were inherently faster. The Board in New Zealand eventually concluded there were sufficient grounds to justify another go and we began to make plans and to liaise with Titouan over a start date.

Our first priority was to organise a refit which would ensure that the boat was strong enough to withstand a second attempt. We had also agreed to tour the fruit-shipping ports of New Zealand to allow the owners, who were the growers, a chance to see their property and enjoy a short sail in her as well. Initial costings showed that if we shipped *Enza*, free of charge, to New Zealand, we could get the refit done there first and make a few additional adjustments which, in the light of the first voyage, we thought might improve performance.

We towed *Enza* down to Tilbury after disentangling her from the buoys which had become confused by a visiting full-sized replica of a Greek trireme which shared our mooring. For a few days our technically advanced sailing vessel lay alongside an example of the ancients' creativity – it made an interesting comparison. Once again I co-opted *Morayshire* for the trip down river. To start work on the boat, and accompany her whilst she was shipped, Angus Buchanan, one of the original shore gang at Hamble, was signed up. He was desperately keen to join the crew and was hopeful of a place for the second voyage.

Whilst Angus and *Enza* travelled to New Zealand, David Alan-Williams was compiling a wish list of modifications. On the first trip the light-wind performance had been disappointing. Indeed an analysis of our performance against *Commodore*'s showed that it was in light conditions when she opened up a lead, whereas in heavy weather we usually clawed back distance. An improvement in this department could be made by reducing weight and wetted surface (the actual area of the hull in contact with the sea, since all such surface provides drag). So David looked at weight, shape and length and had produced some preliminary plans by the time *Enza* arrived in Auckland.

Weight was always uppermost in everyone's minds but it was hard to find any obvious savings except for the dagger boards. These were designed to give grip when the boat was beating to windward, however as the course was mainly downwind, it was decided to dispense with such large boards. New ones were made, both smaller and lighter, to give a weight saving of at least a hundred kilograms per board. Their casings were also restructured to cure the leaking problems of the first attempt. In fact this weight saving was largely cancelled out by a major change to the hulls. We fitted scoops on the sterns which added five feet to the length and overcame the tendency to drag in light conditions. Whilst the hulls were being modified, two feet were added at the bows to give more buoyancy and prevent them nosing into the sea. Throwing vast fountains of water into the air looked impressive but was not achieving anything except to make the boat wetter on deck and cause additional drag. The overall effect of these modifications was to increase the overall length to 92 feet, making *Enza* the largest racing multihull in the world.

The shape of the hulls bothered David since initially they were designed for an 85-footer (with scoops), then cut back to 80, and had five feet of a different shape added for the first voyage and now we were going to add another five feet with the new scoops. Not being decked in, scoops are a way of adding speed-enhancing length without extra weight. In effect we had a 92-foot-long boat which consisted of a number of separate hull units. Since a complete rebuild was not viable, a 60-foot foam-filled section was bonded on beneath each hull and then covered with kevlar. The idea was to give protection against any more UFOs (Unidentified Floating Objects) by creating a double bottom so if we did strike anything, and there was plenty of rubbish around heavy enough to hole the boat, the outer skin might get broken but the inner one should hold. It was also intended to aid performance by providing more rocker to the hulls and a more elliptical shape to the bottom. The new shape moved the centre of buoyancy forward, another advantage as it raised the bows further out of the water. The hulls now looked as if they were designed for 92 feet instead of 80 feet with extensions, and the balance meant there was no need to alter the mast rake or stepping position since there was little actual change in the location of the centre of effort and the centre of lateral resistance.

The living accommodation also received attention. In the godpod the bunks were moved forward to fill an empty void and this left useful space on each side at the aft end. On the port side there was now more storage room and on the other side a small film-editing studio for George was created. Previously his equipment was kept at the foot of my bunk, which made it difficult for him to work if I was asleep, or difficult for me to sleep if he was working. Most of these improvements did not hit one immediately, but the new exterior paint scheme did. Instead of the red and white which had been applied in Hamble, the hulls were now white and covered with giant apples. (The artist had got subversive at one point and included a maggot in one of them. The game was to see how long it took people to find the maggot!) Unkind critics said it looked like a greengrocer's barrow or a fruit salad and you could see their point! One thing was certain, there could be no mistaking what *Enza* was marketing.

The new crew was assembled when I flew out to Auckland in October. There were three changes. Paul Standbridge had left us as Lawrie Smith asked him to join the crew of *Fortuna* for the Whitbread Race before we knew whether we were going again. Paul's acceptance of the definite offer was our loss and Lawrie's gain. He was replaced by two new crew members. Barry McKay was with the *Steinlager 2* and later on the New Zealand America's Cup boat in San Diego. The son of a fisherman, and a boatbuilder by trade, he was a useful addition to the crew. Angus Buchanan had earned his place by dint of hard work and enthusiasm. He had just left Southampton University and was in that period of life where he was wondering what to do next. Since medicine was a likely option, he was told to learn as much as he could about first aid and was put in charge of the medical department.

Undoubtedly, a crew of eight gave us a weight penalty which amounted to perhaps 400–500 kilograms against *Commodore*'s five. But our larger crew gave us the strength to press the boat harder and have more people on watch. With a small crew there is a tendency, when a sail change means calling up someone who might be tired, to put the operation off until a watch change and this can cost a lot of time in a race. While more rest time would equate with fresher thinking on watch or at the helm.

Peter met me at Auckland airport and was full of enthusiasm for the new performance. Initial trials showed that the potential average speed might be up by about two knots and he thought we could easily swish up to 24 knots where we had only achieved 20 before. This was soon to be tested as we were due to start a busy schedule of port visits which would serve as a good shakedown for us and show *Enza* to the apple growers. We departed from Auckland on the 9th October and ran straight into calms which were followed briefly by some strong squalls as we sailed down the east coast of North Island, but nothing really to test the boat properly, though sufficient to delay our arrival at the port of Nelson on the north of South Island until the 13th. We took three parties out that day and nine the next, a punishing schedule, but we learnt as much as our guests did. Producing apples appeared to be almost too easy in the New Zealand climate, which promotes growth at a racing pace compared with Britain, and the concern is not the size of the crop so much as choosing the right mix of varieties. Our publicity potential was a factor fully appreciated by nearly everyone we met. One person did ask why we couldn't start and finish in New Zealand, but saw the light when asked where he wanted to sell his apples!

From Nelson we sailed to Wellington, the capital, in its large protected lagoon north of the Cook Strait. It appeared beautifully sited but was subject to quite vicious squalls, one of which hit as we sailed towards the new marina where we were due to berth. The speed did not build up quickly enough to dissipate the strength of wind so we began to heel and soon the starboard hull left the water and continued to rise as we were caught in relaxed mode and were a bit slow to react and ease the sheets. Still, it gave the local newspapers a dramatic photograph! On the quay were a group of Maori dancers who gave us a traditional *haka* welcome as we came alongside.

Our next stop was Port Lyttleton near Christchurch, where the wooden sailing ship berths shown in so many old photographs still exist, and from there we sailed to Dunedin, the southernmost port of the tour. This enabled me to have a really enjoyable reunion with the three men who had stood by me twenty-five years before when I went aground off the harbour entrance in *Suhaili*. They had anchored close by and waited until the tide rose enough to float me safely off. We have kept in touch over the years and the last time we met was in 1977 when I flew down during the Auckland stopover of the Whitbread Race.

We sailed out from Otago just ahead of a front with lovely strong winds from the south-west. This gave a real test of the boat's performance and 32.3 knots was reached whilst Brian Aitken was on the helm. Since he was the one who had to justify all the expenses this seemed tactful! In the middle of the excitement George wandered up from below, took one look at the muddle of empty mugs in the cockpit, and said, "Those little mugs don't look as if they've seen a tea bag for a while", collected the empties and carried them off for a refill. New Zealanders seem to be great tea-drinkers, and I suspect the gallonage of tea consumed there exceeds that of beer by a very large margin, so with our mixed Brit and Kiwi crew there were always ready customers whenever someone suggested putting the kettle on.

Our next stop was Napier back on North Island, a rich agricultural region famous for its wine where it appeared anything would grow. We had some lovely sailing across the bay with yet more growers, followed by a cracking party at the yacht club. Unfortunately, I had to leave at this point to return to London, so I missed the last port before Auckland and the awaiting P & O container ship. Sadly, the schedule had not allowed time for exploration inland but there is a case for always leaving something desirable unseen to encourage you to return again. On the whole it had been a most pleasant interlude but the best news was that *Enza* was definitely faster and we felt confident in projecting a target for a circumnavigation of seventy-seven days, even though it meant the average speed required would rise to 14.74 knots, over half a knot more than last time. It was a tall order, but then getting round in one piece in under eighty days required more than a little good fortune anyway.

The news that greeted me on my return home was that Titouan had fallen out of the race. Apparently, in spite of all his high hopes the arguments over his boat damage still raged and repairs had not even started. We were now committed to going, but lack of competition would remove much of the spice from the voyage without the giant monohull/multihull confrontation. Then we learned that Olivier de Kersuason had found a new sponsor, the French water utility, Lyonnaise des Eaux-Dumez, and with their support was going again, but this time he was keen to have competition. Contact was established and since it benefited both parties, we agreed to start together and make a race of it. Olivier flew over and we met at Netley Lodge near Southampton to discuss the rules. He still refused to join the Jules Verne Association and at every opportunity was slagging it off and the people involved, from French cabinet ministers down, in his own inimitable style. However, he was quite prepared to go through the Association's start and finish line, although for the media's benefit he wanted an additional line closer in to Brest that could be observed easily from the land. So the course was set: the start line for the race against Olivier was at the entrance to the roadstead at Brest, then out to the Jules Verne start off Ushant then round the world and back again across the same two finish lines. Olivier insisted he was allowed to stop and take on supplies or seek assistance, if he so wished, but agreed that, if he did, the clock would keep ticking. The point of the whole event was the excitement of boat against boat and the winner must be the first home and not judged after a long wait whilst 'injury time' ran out for one or the other.

The only issue left was a start date. Early in the New Year once more suited everyone and we agreed to go on stand-by for the first favourable weather forecast after the 4th January 1994. Routiers were to be allowed. Olivier intended using the French Navy meteorologists and we had Bob Rice in the USA. This time round we felt no qualms about having this assistance, since Bruno had employed it throughout last time and it was permitted under the rules. The fact that we had rival routiers added an interesting dimension as, if the boats turned out to have a near equal performance, the accuracy of the routing information could be decisive.

Even if she was unable to complete a circumnavigation on her own keel in 1993, *Enza* did get around the world as deck cargo as the large container ships use the Cape Horn route. She went out to New Zealand via the Cape of Good Hope and came home to Tilbury via Cape Horn. We hoped she would make this a habit! We stepped the mast in the docks and then *Morayshire* towed us down river into the Thames estuary. Although the wind was light when we cast off the tow just after passing the Nore, we were soon trundling along at 11 knots, destination Hamble. All the storing procedures were a repeat of the previous year – dehydrated food packed into weekly containers, spares checked and stowed, fuel for the generators and heater, some seventy-five gallons in total. Experiments using the parties of growers as mobile ballast in New Zealand had shown there was a definite increase in speed when weight was moved aft, so we stowed all the fuel and heavy stores right at the stern.

A voyage around the world concentrates the mind wonderfully for some people and before we sailed David got married and Barry became engaged. Peter took a distinctly jaundiced view of these joyful events, convinced it would mean neither would have their minds on the boat and sailing. Good crewmen aboard *Steinlager*, he said, went to pot when they married during the previous Whitbread. Everyone away from family has some feelings of anxiety and, in view of the new relationships, it was not surprising that we experienced a heavy increase in radio and telex traffic, though none of us was guiltless on that score – least of all Peter himself!

6

Slingshot Down the Atlantic

On the 16th January 1994 the two competitors were on their marks for what was billed as the planetary match race between the world's largest trimaran and catamaran. Both boats had received major refits since their respective mishaps the previous year, so comparisons between the earlier performances were no longer strictly relevant. Nevertheless our catamaran had appeared to be the faster craft, insofar as we had gained on the trimaran over the three weeks we were racing. We believed the improvements had given us a greatly enhanced boat but theirs was an unknown factor. Both crews were veterans now and had learned much from the preceding bid and, having failed once, had everything to prove. Above all, each of us thought we could win.

From the beginning of January Bob Rice produced daily forecasts and projections for the following ten days. Meteorology used to be rather a black art but satellite photographs have helped immeasurably to aid forecasting and it is now a more precise science. We kept in touch daily but nothing likely appeared during the first week of January. The second week of the New Year did not look too promising either but Bob warned there just might be a chance of northerly winds about the middle of the month. As before, the forecaster's task was not only to find us a northerly wind for the first 300 miles across the Bay of Biscay, it had to be a northerly that continued down the Portuguese coast as well. There were one or two good northerlies in the English Channel but these occurred when there were south-westerlies in the Finisterre and Trafalgar forecast areas which span the west coast of Spain and Portugal, and there was no point in rushing across the Bay of Biscay only to come to a grinding halt once we reached the opposite corner at Cape Finisterre. We needed luck to get round in seventy-seven days, and there was no point in overloading this unpredictable little lady right at the outset.

As it happened it was just as well the weather prevented the race starting early in January because we would have been alone. *Lyonnaise des Eaux-Dumez* (ex-*Charal*) was trapped ashore in her shed by the high winds on the 4th and was only launched when the gales abated. This left little time for trials but the French seemed happy enough with the boat and were keen to get going. By the 14th the forecast for the Bay of Biscay and the Channel was awful, gales everywhere, but Bob thought the south-westerlies would back round to the east and then north-east or north and this system was bringing a favourable change down the Portuguese coast as well. We could have sat around for months waiting for anything as attractive. A quick call to Olivier de Kersuason confirmed that his routiers were also watching the approaching pattern and saw the possible window of opportunity too, so we put out a call for the crew to muster.

We were towed from Hamble into the Solent shortly before 2200 hours on the 14th in a light south-westerly. Portland and Plymouth sea areas were forecast to have southerly winds of force 6, becoming cyclonic, the Bay of Biscay was giving south-westerly force 6 to 8, becoming westerly 8 to 9, a severe gale. Normally, no one in their right mind goes to sea with this sort of forecast, but Bob stuck to his prognosis, so off we went. In fact the strongest wind we met all the way across the Channel was force 5 and whilst we were on passage the wind did begin to back round through south. We sailed into Brest harbour at 4 am on the 16th with a force 4 from the north-north-east and strengthening winds promised, and moored at Moulin Blanc Marina, as before, but this time astern of *Lyonnaise des Eaux-Dumez* instead of *Commodore*. At first glance, apart from the name, the boat did not appear to have changed very much, but she looked ready to sail.

The weather omens were still looking good and Bob was insistent that we seize the opening quickly, since he did not think it would last for long. Tow boats were ordered to take us out of the Marina at 8 am. Those of the crew who had wives present went ashore for a last farewell. This did not include me as Sue had not come across to

France. She does not like these farewells and, to be honest, I prefer to concentrate on the boat just before departure. But I put through a quick call to say we would be off shortly, then turned in to my bunk onboard. I remembered I should have told Sue to put money on us at Ladbrokes who were offering odds of 7–4, but of course I forgot!

Zodiac inflatables arrived promptly at 8 am and we were towed backwards from the berth into the approach channel where a launch took over. As we proceeded towards the harbour we passed all spare equipment such as fenders and mooring lines to the Zodiacs to be stored pending our return. They were surplus weight since there were no plans to tie up anywhere before we returned and, if it did become necessary for any reason, the lack of lines and fenders would be the least of our worries. This was the second attempt and it must be successful – there would certainly be no third chance.

Both boats were held under tow in the bay whilst a submarine came into port. Brest is a naval harbour and the French Navy closes the entrance channel whenever they have a warship entering or leaving. Some spectator craft accompanied us, the largest being a French frigate, but it was very chilly for those who were not wrapped up well, as the wind was now a cold north-north-east force 6 – just perfect for sailors who wanted to sail fast to the south-west!

The first start line marking the beginning of the match race was between the middle ground mark in the channel and the fort on the north shore. We timed ourselves down well and made a good start, over a minute ahead of *Lyonnaise* and increased this slightly as we sailed out westward on a fine reach. This was the easy bit as we were still sheltered by the land but once we moved out clear of Basse St Pierre and were exposed to the full strength of the wind, the seas became very lumpy. We had debated whether to beat up inside Ushant through the Canal du Four but this entailed tacking against an adverse tide. Progress would have been slow and manoeuvring room was limited in the channel by rocks, so we decided to round Ushant Island from the south. Peter took the helm whilst I navigated, sailing as close to the rocks on the north side as we dared to keep the fetch, and therefore the wave size, down. This brought us well-intentioned advice on the radio from a spectator craft behind who did not have the benefit of a Global Positioning System (GPS) and thought we were cutting things a bit fine. I knew otherwise, nevertheless I was glad when they found conditions too rough and turned away, since they were like back-seat drivers and there is nothing worse than constant interruptions when one is concentrating.

The waves were horrendous and would have done credit to seventeenth- and eighteenth-century marine artists. *Enza* was leaping out of the sea in some of the shortest and steepest green waves I have ever experienced. Trying to plot on the chart was almost impossible as the boat shuddered at each impact with the waves throwing anything loose into the air. One crash was so ferocious it dislodged the compass from its base and tore out the lighting cables with the force of the jump. With blows like this we would need to check the stowage of all the stores later, assuming nothing serious was broken in the meantime. Behind us we could see *Lyonnaise* suffering in the same way and showing all her anti-fouling paint on the hull bottoms at times. Both of us were well reefed, but even so we were over-pressed and changed a headsail. Whilst this was happening *Lyonnaise* overtook us to leeward and took a small but significant PR lead.

We were coming into the Jules Verne start line from the west and one could not help reflecting that if it had been in Brest harbour, life would have been easier for everyone and avoided this unpleasant bouncing beat, but Ushant was the accepted line internationally and to this mark we had to make our way. Being ahead, *Lyonnaise* was able to tack eastwards before us and we saw her swing round as she passed over the mark and suddenly grow rapidly in size as she rushed back towards us, enjoying a broad reach and overtaking a labouring cargo ship in perfect high-speed sailing conditions. Her time on the line was 1253. Those lucky bastards, they would already be drying out and feeling warmer, whilst we bashed on for another seven minutes. We watched enviously as she swept past but our turn was coming. I made radio contact with David Pelly of the World Sailing Speed Record Council who had us in sight from the lighthouse on Ushant Island where he would take our time officially. We overstood to the east slightly so we could cross the start line at full speed, then we wore round, trimmed the sails and were off again. The wind, force 7, gave us surfing conditions at an average speed of 20 knots. The greatest sail of our lives had started.

Where was *Lyonnaise*? In just eight minutes she was already nearly three miles away and barely visible. Instead of following in her track we set the best course for our boat and gradually diverged, as she was steering slightly more to the north of the rhumb line, the direct course for a point just west of Cape Finisterre. *Lyonnaise* had a very baggy genoa/spinnaker set and we responded by putting up a spinnaker which was more efficient as we were achieving the same speed but on a course further off the wind. After two hours we were so far apart that we lost sight of her to the north, but this put us closer to the next mark, and so in the lead. Naturally the performances of the two boats during these first few hours gave little indication as to how the race might go overall but we were pleased with the way things were developing. We had reached better whilst in the sheltered waters of the harbour entrance, but she had the advantage in rough conditions when sailing close to the wind. Now in order to keep up whilst further away from the rhumb line, or make wider zigzags, *Lyonnaise* needed greater speed and the fact that she was now bearing north showed she was not succeeding in this respect anyway. Still, at this stage when everyone and everything was settling down, it was too early to draw any firm conclusions.

Once we had the sails trimmed to optimum effect we began to recover from the bash to the start line. The food boxes had been thrown around and the tools and spares were all over the place. Sorting this out gave Ed an opportunity to search for excess weight, a major preoccupation as the days passed. In fact anyone standing still for more than a few seconds ran the risk of being threatened with instant jettisoning! Remembering that everything except the sails add to the weight, nothing was safe and there were yells of glee when he unearthed the padlocks used to seal the boat in port and chucked them overside. Three pounds lighter we tore on. A few days later in what may have been an attempt to follow Ed's example, George failed to hold on to the frying pan properly when washing up and it dropped into the sea. We carried no spares in this department so fry-ups became an item to be crossed off the list of treats. This was a bad day for George as the duty cook went down to see how the spaghetti sauce was coming along, having already mixed it with water to give plenty of time for reconstitution, but could not find it anywhere. Then someone

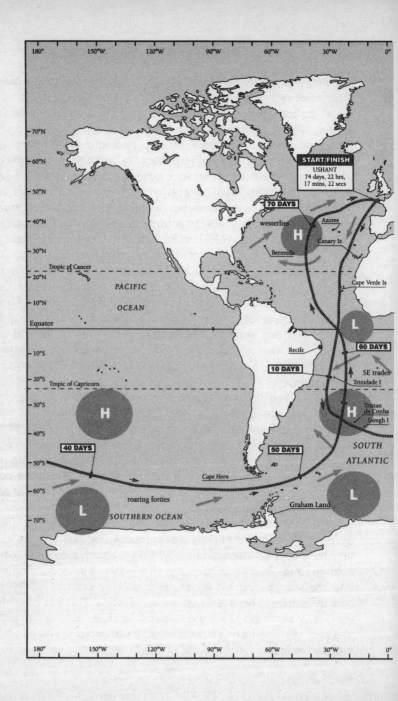

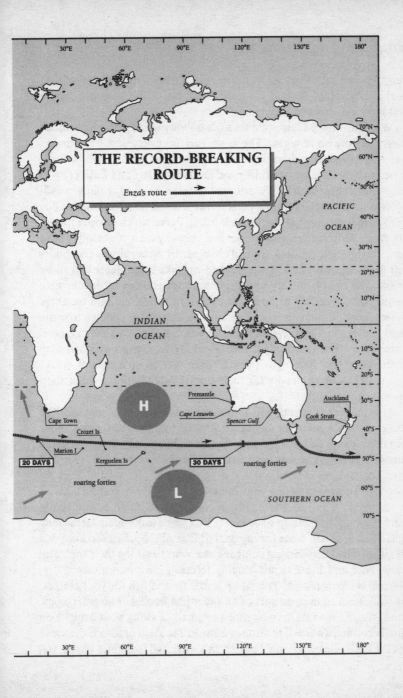

remembered that George had done the previous meal's washing up and it transpired he had assumed the mess in the saucepan was a leftover and chucked it overside!

We went straight into watches since nobody managed to have much sleep the previous night. The start had been exciting but energy-sapping as well and although it was hard to leave the centre of activity when progress was so sparkling, we needed an alert and fresh crew to maintain the pressure. We adopted a three-on-duty, rolling watch system where each hour one person was relieved by a fresh hand. The objective was to avoid the usual learning curve which happens when an entire watch is changed at once and this way we would always have sufficient people on deck for sail changes. In theory it was five hours off and three on but it never worked out like this. Meals had to be made, the boat kept tidy and there were times when all hands were required to speed up a particular evolution. For Peter and me there were the additional chores of radio schedules, plus updates to write and fax home. The crew decided the watch system was the skippers' attempt to test their limited mental ability to figure out when they were on watch. As Angus put it, "There are so many alarm clocks going off to wake people for their turn, it sounds like a clock shop gone wrong!"

It is the watch system which dominates life aboard a boat, not the times of meals, noon, or any other familiar routines. You rarely wake for daybreak, you wake for your watch, night and day, rough or calm, hot or freezing, The words cruelly whispered in your ear, "It's ten to" or "Ten minutes to your watch", drag you rudely from your sleep. As consciousness is regained your bunk has never felt so comfortable or your sleeping bag so warm. Just a couple more minutes, you think, and begin to drift asleep once more. You jerk awake again. How long have I dozed? Am I late for my watch? One of the greatest crimes in a boat is to be late relieving someone else who has done their trick and now, cold and tired, is just longing to crawl back into a warm, dry, sprayless environment. You sit up hurriedly and fish for your clothes, usually stacked in some sort of an order just in case of an emergency, and struggle into them in a space too small to swing your arms. You are becoming aware of the noises outside, the slash of spray, the swish of the hulls, the occasional bang from a wave and indistinct voices. If it is wet outside you have to beware of putting a nice dry besocked foot into a puddle of water that has dripped from your caller's oilskins. You look for your oilies and struggle to put your feet through trousers into boots that have been left strapped tightly to the bottom of the legs. This reduces two actions into one and the chances are you will put the boots on the right way round. The boots are damp, the inside of trousers and jacket cold and clammy. You pull the hood on (twenty-five per cent of the heat lost from a body is lost through the head), tighten the neck flap and do up the safety harness. Then you crawl from the dimly lit cabin out into the watery pitch black of the cockpit. If the others are kind a mug of tea awaits, which you clutch gratefully as you absorb the scene on deck: the course, wind, sea state, sails set, trim, who is on the helm, how's she feeling, are we going as fast as possible? Then you slump down on the cockpit coaming, back to the spray, but your mind is getting into gear. Soon you are engrossed with the tactics of weather-routing, like a chess player thinking of the moves you will be make two days from now, perhaps 900 miles from here, and where precisely to steer the boat to gain the most favourable winds then. The first hour crawls by and you take the helm as a new face joins the cockpit and someone else departs. This is usually the excuse for another brew, a discreet conversation, but the eyes never leave the instruments glowing dimly before the wheel, watching the speed and feeling the waves as the boat hurtles forwards. One more hour and then it's your turn to creep below, write the log, check the Satcom to see if there is any news in and then undress and snuggle into the sleeping bag. Another three hours of your life have passed, another sixty miles of the voyage accomplished.

The forecasts for Biscay and Finisterre were both northerly force 6–8, easing to force 5 later. This was almost perfect. We had hoped for a slingshot out across the bay and down the Portuguese coast and it looked as if this would materialise. Surfs of up to 29 knots were already occurring and we had to shut from our minds any thoughts of collisions with the large and heavy logs which frequently litter this area. Logs are probably the most dangerous flotsam since they float indefinitely, but they were a hazard we just had to ignore or we would never break the record. We crashed on. By midnight the average speed had fallen slightly to 18.72 knots and the wind was down to an estimated force 6 (the masthead windvane had ceased to function properly so we were not sure). With the illumination from a powerful torch we could see it hanging drunkenly at the masthead, no doubt loosened by the terrible bashing on the way to Ushant. In the morning Jaws was hauled aloft to fit the spare, an unpleasant task whilst we were surging, as any small jar is magnified enormously by the height of the mast. At the top there is the danger of air sickness but during the ascent the force of the boat bouncing around can easily dislodge a person and send him swinging like a pendulum with the possibility of broken bones. To prevent this we organised another halyard on the outside of the mast as a handhold for Jaws, as the mast itself had too great a diameter for him to wrap his arms around properly.

Our first day at sea in fast reaching conditions proved beyond all doubt that all the modifications were really worthwhile. No longer did the bows spoon up nearly every sea and throw it backwards across the deck because the additional buoyancy forward lifted the front of the boat sufficiently to prevent most of the burying that had occurred before. As a result life was more agreeable for those on deck and going forward no longer guaranteed a soaking. It also meant there was less resistance from the structure to its passage through the water, a small contribution to promote speed.

One improvement that had crept past the accountants was two large waterproof loudspeakers that played into the cockpit from a tape-player in the godpod. However, it was one thing having the ability to give ourselves musical accompaniment as we raced along, quite another to agree on what should be played. It was this more than anything that showed the generation gap in our crew. I like classical music, musicals and sixties rock and roll. Peter's tastes were not very different. But with the youngsters it was instant war. If I put on Delibes it would suddenly be replaced by cacophony. I asked what it was.

"Crowded House," said Angus.

"I didn't ask where it was recorded," I responded tetchily, as I switched tapes again. Barry leaned into the godpod and, muttering to the others "This will fix him", switched to something called Buzzcocks which threatened to lift the lid off the cabin. I went implacably back to Delibes – but louder. Angus suffered this for a while and then asked plaintively if we could have a change. We compromised on *Cats*.

The first real indication of how we were faring against *Lyonnaise* came shortly after 11 am on the 17th when we had been racing for twenty-two hours from Ushant. She had covered 360 miles and was further south and east of us. This confirmed their policy was to tack downwind, so she was actually sailing faster, but the zigzags meant her mileage was not converting as well into straight distance covered along the course. Our position at the same time put us 378 miles from the start line and on a southerly course as we were already west of Finisterre. Three and a half hours later when we were west of Vigo we sighted a sail to our east steering south by west at 21 knots. The sail slowly moved towards us and passed about three miles astern, so we had no difficulty in recognising *Lyonnaise* steering a more westerly course, not that there were likely to be any other craft around doing this sort of speed. As we were crossing tracks we both overtook a merchant ship which must have wondered what on earth was going on. *Lyonnaise* had closed sixteen miles in four hours, so either her earlier position was inaccurate or she had sailed at 24 knots for the last four hours. Her speed relative to us did not look like 24 knots so we assumed the earlier position was confused in transmission! What was significant however was the closeness of the two boats after about 440 miles and, if either boat believed they were in for an easy ride, this meeting showed otherwise. The alterations to *Lyonnaise* were obviously very effective and although it was nice to be ahead, a gap of three miles was nothing and we could not afford to relax for a moment if we wished to maintain our lead. We exchanged brief greetings.

The wind freshened during the afternoon and was hovering at a full gale by midnight. We changed from the spinnaker to the jib top at 8 pm as the wind and seas rose, all hands on deck for the job to ensure it went smoothly. Once set, we goose-winged it out on the opposite side to the mainsail so we sailed more or less straight downwind towards the next objective, a waypoint just west of the Canary Islands. We could now safely assume we were into the north-east trade winds, the second stage of the weather route we had to tackle. The speed fell slightly with the reduced sail area but the boat was happy, averaging 17 knots even though the crew on watch in the cockpit were subjected to the occasional rogue wave dropping on to them. Oilskins were essential to avoid soaking our inner clothing, a matter of some concern since we had all reduced wardrobes to save weight. Once clothing is soaked in salt water it must be thoroughly washed in fresh or it will never dry properly and there was not sufficient fresh water to launder clothing.

We had all hands out again at 5 am the next morning when we gybed. No risks this time, the main was reduced right down to the third reef and then let out to the first reef afterwards. It was whilst tidying the reefing lines in the forward cockpit (known as the snake pit because however often it was squared away, all the halyards stored there soon broke loose and resembled a seething mass of snakes) that I was given a salutary reminder of the dangers aboard a relatively small boat. We came down on to a wave, the sea shot up through the net floor as if it were non-existent and gently lifted and carried me aft along with it. It was incredibly comfortable, which is perhaps why I was not as alarmed as perhaps I should have been. Fortunately, the boat rose, the water dropped away and I was deposited in the middle of the coach roof just in front of Ed.

"Thanks for protecting me from the wave," he said as I scrambled to a sitting position.

"The things we do for you youngsters," I responded, whilst discovering to my relief that no water had found its way down my neck.

As on the previous day, we received a position from *Lyonnaise* during the morning. She was about a degree to the south but more than two degrees east and so still tacking downwind. Bob Rice had instructed us to head out to the west as the winds were easing close to the African coastline and we were following this advice. If he was right, *Lyonnaise*, who might appear to have a slight lead at the moment, could well lose it during the next day. This proved to be the case, as the next morning, the third day at sea, they were almost on the same longitude but about ten miles behind.

As we moved steadily south into warmer climes, flying fish and Portuguese men-of-war were already being sighted. The fish are not large, the big ones are rarely more than half a kilo or so, and they rely upon an extended pectoral fin to enable them to leap out of the water and glide away from danger. The shadow of a boat looks dangerous to them, so we were often surrounded by gliding fish. Usually, they escaped but some came at or over the boat, and the thump of a fish hitting the hull was quite normal. The larger ones can be quite a menace as they ascend ten feet or more from the surface and fly across the deck at considerable speed at head height. If they strike the body it is painful and those that hit the face really hurt.

In the first three days *Enza* covered 1,272 miles, *Lyonnaise* perhaps a dozen less. This put us both well ahead of the 354 daily average required for a seventy-seven-day circumnavigation and we had established a cushion already of over 200 miles, or more than half a day. On the previous attempt we reached the Canary Islands in three and a half days, which had seemed amazingly fast, but this time it took six hours less. Steve Anscell rushed out to the islands to overfly us and collect the microwaved film taken so far. We had the facilities to inspect film on board before sending it off and some of the shots George took at the start, when we were bashing between Brest and Ushant, made you seasick just to look at them. We wondered how the spectacular lurches would look on a large screen.

Learning from the previous experience we took a course well west of the Canary Islands to avoid the wind shadow created in their lee. Our speeds were increasing, reaching 465 miles during the fourth day when we had the breakthrough we were seeking against *Lyonnaise*. She suddenly dropped back over 120 miles, a huge differential in so short a time, which we could only attribute to being caught in the Canary Islands wind shadow zones. The report from the boat explained the slow progress was due to tiredness as none of the crew had been off deck since the start. If this were true they were not pacing themselves too intelligently.

There is a strange tendency amongst sailors to make extravagant claims for the periods they have managed without sleep. The most extreme I have heard is twelve days, which was utter nonsense, of course. My personal longest is just over three days and that led to my going aground off Dunedin, the origin of my recent happy reunion. It happened because I was not analysing things properly. I received a boost of adrenalin from the incident but it quickly wore off, leaving me totally exhausted. Even though I was twenty-nine years old and extremely fit, I know I could not have continued to function efficiently for much longer and it taught me to pace myself in future and try always to leave energy in reserve for emergencies. If the *Lyonnaise* crew had really been awake for three days, then it was not surprising they lost so much ground. Now, if ever, was the moment to pile on the pressure. We managed 490 miles the next day to *Lyonnaise*'s 460, a far from tardy performance by the exhausted Frenchmen. What made these speeds all the more impressive was that both boats were fully loaded with nearly three months of stores and could expect to sail even faster as these were consumed.

We swept past the Cape Verde Islands during the next day. The wind veered round to the east a touch so we were broad reaching rather than running with the wind, which was a steady force 5–6. Because of the sea state we set a speed limit of 28 knots, but David was soon swooping down waves well in excess of this and since speeding tickets had no effect, he was threatened – and incurred – porridge duty. When he appeared impervious to all threats we took in a reef. These were perfect conditions for *Enza* and we took full advantage. In the twenty-four hours from 7 am on the 21st January we covered 520.9 miles, which created a new world record. In recent years claims have been made for greater distances within twenty-four hours but none were based on an independent automatic polling system linked to a GPS and most were interpolations calculated between positions which could not be independently checked. We carried a polling system built into our Satcom C communication equipment which could be switched to sending an automatic reading of the GPS position at any interval we chose. We had set it for hourly intervals whilst we were rushing down the trade winds so our claim for a new world record could be substantiated. It may seem a little unfair to earlier sailors that their claims will go unrecognised because the equipment to give an independent check has only recently been invented, but one must remember they were unable to measure or prove the distance precisely anyway. This phenomenal burst of speed meant we had sailed more than a thousand nautical miles in two days. How the old square-riggers would have loved to have knocked off distances like that. Come to think about it, how I would have loved to have done it twenty-five years ago. Records are, of course, there to be beaten and ours lasted only five months, being exceeded by Frenchman Laurent

Bourgnon, in the 60-foot trimaran *Primagaz*, who achieved a remarkable twenty-four-hour run of 538.7 miles.

Our record run was accomplished without one of the big spinnakers which had earlier torn across at its head. Wear and tear on sails is to be expected when the sort of forces which might be withstood for a few hours in the Solent races are continued for days on end, but this sail should not have torn where it was reinforced. It was a weak link and we were fortunate to recover the pieces without further damage because when a lightweight nylon sail goes into the water there is every chance it will become entangled on the dagger boards or rudders or get torn on the log transducers. This time we were lucky and, apart from the tear at the top, we had a simple panel rip to sew. Barry started the job and was soon joined by a large team working away in relays on and off watch. Apart from this he was being kept busy and had already used his famous DIY skills to repair the main traveller, the car which slides from side to side on a track across the boat and allows the mainsail to be adjusted. A bolt within the car had come loose and stuck between the car and the track, thus jamming the whole system. It took a couple of hours to fix. In long-distance sailing the crew must be competent mechanics and electricians, as well as good sailors, since there are no boatyards to telephone for help when things go wrong.

Sometimes, however, a very minor problem could grow out of all proportion. David had a spinnaker sheet turning block just above his bunk that squeaked. The repetitive noise kept him from sleeping, so he went up on deck to pour water on it. Jaws, who shared the same cabin, suggested that the best solution would be to change the block. Peter put a rolling hitch on the sheet to hold it whilst this operation was taking place but found he had used the tail of the sheet itself, so another restraint had to be found. By this time there was a spider's web of lines and the wrong one got let off, so the sheet ran out with Peter and David trying to hold on. They might as well have tried to stop the tides and David's finger became trapped in the block. Eventually the problem was resolved and a new non-squeaking block was in place, but David did not get any sleep anyway because now he was kept awake by a throbbing finger.

Our headlong rush southwards now brought us close to the inter-tropical convergence zone, but there was no let-up in the trade winds. We spoke on the radio to a passing French merchant ship heading the other way who informed us that he had had north-north-easterly winds of force 4–5 for the past day, which told us there were no calms at least until the equator. It also confirmed Bob Rice's projections and he was now predicting we might thunder through the area usually occupied by the doldrums without pause – the convergence zone seemed to have disappeared! The choice of longitude when crossing the equator is of fundamental importance, since even a small delay from light winds, which might reduce our speed to 8 knots, meant the loss of 160 miles a day on the required average of 14.74 knots. When drawing up the schedule of daily averages needed to achieve the target, I allowed for a drop in speed in this vicinity and we had to cover only 180 miles a day over two of the days we anticipated being in lighter winds (see Appendix I). Thus a drop to 8 knots would not be disastrous, but how much better to maintain a higher average and put miles into the bank. On the first attempt we were only too aware of being too far east where the convergence zone, and therefore the area of calms, is wider, with the result we had watched *Commodore* sweep past us at 26°W. This time Bob Rice guided us towards a point about 27°W to cross into the southern hemisphere and this agreed with our instincts.

Apart from seasonal variations, the world's wind patterns do not really change much and there is a great deal of information to be derived from the study of old records from the days before vessels had engines and depended entirely on wind. The square-riggers, heavy and under-canvassed compared with a modern yacht, could take ages to pass through the doldrums, with some being delayed for up to two months. A century ago the famous Flying P Line of Hamburg, who ran a highly efficient sailing ship service between Hamburg and the west coast of South America, took immense trouble to examine their captains' routes and performances. This led to instructions being issued that their vessels were to aim for a point between 26°–28°W when crossing the equator outward bound, since that was where, on average, the most consistent winds would be found. Significantly, the Flying P Line was able to average one and a half round voyages a year, as opposed to the one of their competitors, and they stayed in business with sailing vessels right into the 1920s. Such was their confidence in sail that in 1926 they ordered a new engineless barque, the *Padua*, the last pure sailing commercial square-rigger built, and still sailing today as the training ship *Krusenstern*. These tough ships and hard men paid no attention to the seasons and rounded the Horn, east and west, to suit the cargoes not the weather. But they were 5,000 tons or more, not a tiny ten tons like_us!

It appeared we had been extraordinarily lucky crossing through the doldrums, and now, like all sailors since the early Portuguese mariners, we were watching for a change in the wind direction to show us we were in the south-east trades. During the evening of the 22rd January the wind began to ease from force 5–6 and veer from the north-east. This was a sign but could not be taken as definite, as the zone moves around. Rain squalls arrived shortly after midnight when we were still 3°30′ N. By daybreak (at 6 am in these latitudes) the wind was east-north-easterly, force 2, the latitude 2°20′N and speed was dropping. We continued to meet squalls of wind up to 20 knots though, and the wind veered sharply in these. Shortly after noon, when our latitude was just over 1° N, the wind veered in a squall again but this time when the rain departed, it remained south-east, force 4. We held our breath and crashed on, taking a course to give a fast reach. Southing was everything now to put space between us and the ITCZ and avoid being pounced on if it moved south. But the wind held and, although our day's run fell below 400 miles for the first time, it was a respectable 388.

At 1724 hours on the 23rd January the two GPSs showed all the zeros in the latitude section, whilst longitude increased to nearly 28° W. The distance travelled from Ushant was 3,223.5 nautical miles and it had taken us 7 days, 4 hours and 24 minutes at an average speed of 18.706 knots, a full thirty-nine hours faster than *Commodore*'s time and a new sailing ship world record.

Whilst we tried to dodge distractions, one aspect of crossing the equator could not be ignored, Angus's initiation. Despite the fact he had ́crossed the line aboard the container vessel taking *Enza* to New Zealand, he was not considered to have been initiated properly. Neptune's Court gathered to receive him, though the ceremony this time lacked the element of drama Paul Standbridge had managed to inject into proceedings. To make the occasion I spent some time creating a chicken curry for dinner that evening which was, as far as I was concerned anyway, meant to be a major treat and not a continuation of Angus's initiation!

Meanwhile the wind continued to be steady, perhaps due to Angus's propitiation of Neptune. On the programme I had allowed nine and a half days to the equator, so we were already over two days ahead of schedule and now we held a course to the south-west, still following the traditional route. In theory this easterly wind should back round through north until we were to the south of the high, where the wind is from the west, sliding smoothly therefore from the Atlantic circulation into the Southern Ocean. Apart from sailing in more favourable winds there are other benefits from following this pattern. The oceanic currents flow with the winds and can give at least half a knot of speed and we were not prepared to turn up our noses at anything which helped us along.

Lyonnaise had dropped behind a little, but it looked as if this was probably only temporary. She came across the equator the next morning after us but ahead of *Commodore*'s record as well. She was demonstrating how improved she was to last year and was only a hundred miles behind, slightly to the west at the moment, and giving little away. The tightness of the racing gave no chance for relaxation, indeed they could well close up during the next section of the race where the winds would be from nearer ahead, a situation which might suit them since the perceived wisdom is that trimarans sail better to windward than catamarans.

Angus had reason to be aggrieved that night when a flying fish caught him on the chest. Surely having been accepted into Neptune's kingdom he should be immune to such treatment? Obviously not, and he went off to change his shirt. He would have to hope for a good rain squall now to wash away the fishy smell. A day before he would not have cared, as we were still wearing oilskins. The weather had been cold and the sky overcast all the way from the English Channel to the equator, so nobody had had an opportunity to build up a sun tan for protection as we moved into hotter climes. The temperature was rising and we had yet to pass beneath the sun, which was lying over 17°S.

As our course took us in towards land it created another opening to send back film and Steve Anscell flew out the next day. We were over 300 miles out to sea but there was no guarantee we would come any closer, since we had to take whatever course best suited the wind, so Steve took the bird in the hand. He flew up from Recife to the small Brazilian Air Force base at Fernando de Noronha where the aircraft was refuelled. The plane was a Navahoe with additional wing tanks to provide the necessary range, but its flying time was only six hours, and at one minute past six hours the engines worked on air. Thus equipped, he and his crew committed themselves to a long flight over the sea which gave them, at best, half an hour overhead, assuming they found us immediately. The pilot was blessed with the unlikely name of Omar Khayyam and although he claimed his grandfather was English, he spoke not a work of the language so an interpreter, who turned out to be a male ballet dancer, was taken along as well. Ten minutes were wasted in the search but it was a miracle they saw us so quickly. The tightness of the schedule meant we could not send all the film George had prepared, but we did what we could in the time and I began to wonder who was taking the greater risks in this whole adventure, Steve or us. It was intended for Steve to fly out again and rendezvous with *Lyonnaise* to receive film from them but Olivier declined to give a position that day so the second trip was cancelled, much to Steve's relief.

We now had to concentrate on the next tactical hurdle, how to get ourselves past the dreaded South Atlantic high pressure centre which was wandering around at about 30°S. This was not a good place to have a gamble as, whatever happened, we had to avoid becoming caught within the centre itself, or any ridges extending from it, as therein would lie calms. Negotiating around one of the Atlantic calm zones would make a perfect board game, the Joker being the movement of the high centre.

Bob Rice was watching the high on satellite images, as were we on the rather uninformative weatherfaxes we received. The South Atlantic is not as highly populated as the north and the result is that there are fewer weather reporting stations and ships and so less information on which to base a forecast. Initial reports put the centre at 38°S and 18°W, which was not good and meant a long detour south. Bob was suggesting we keep to a narrow band of longitude between 30°–32°W and head south through this for the moment, as it contained a funnel of good winds. Certainly on the 25th we achieved a day's run of 419 miles with a largely easterly wind which brought us through 11°S and into an area of squalls which could be seen for miles, in direct contrast to the sunny sparkling blue seas. Cool, heavy rain fell beneath great towering black clouds of cumulus extending right down to the sea's surface, which both refreshed us and cleaned the accumulated salt off the boat, sails and rigging. These clouds contained individual wind systems, heading us on the northern sides and freeing us to the south. As each came close we reduced sail and waited for the gust. The trick was to leave as much sail set as possible until the last minute but not get caught with too much when the wind increased. Even so, these squalls cost time and pushed us slightly west so our day's run was the worst so far, 380 miles.

Trinidade Island, which we actually saw twelve months before, was over a hundred miles to the east this year and we were conscious it was in this area that the starboard dagger board struck an object and lost its lower tip. We were somewhat concerned therefore when a twenty-five-foot pilot whale surfaced about 300 feet away and then raced in towards us. It pulled up about fifteen feet from the port hull and cruised parallel to us. What did it want? Was it one of its friends who damaged us the year before? We would never know, but at twenty-five to thirty tons it was a very heavy object and to be treated with respect. It is possible that we surprised it, as whales sleep on the surface and do not always hear a yacht approaching. Because they meld into the waves they are difficult for humans to spot in a grey sea or at night. Some time ago a friend who was single-handing was awakened by the boat being heaved about and found a whale cuddling up to the hull in what he described as a very amorous manner. This one was probably just plain curious. I don't suppose it saw many yachts, especially with two hulls. He swam along with us for a few minutes more, then dived beneath the hulls and disappeared, much to our relief. Two days later another visitor swam around the boat during the night, intrigued by a torch shining into the water, but luckily he kept clear as well.

On the 27th we passed through 25°S with another day's run below 400 miles, this time of 395, which was disappointing since expectations were now high, but it was still forty miles above the daily average required. We were now south of the sun but it was hot on deck and this caused Olivier aboard *Lyonnaise* to complain that the only thing missing was the flies! He soon had other things to worry about when the exchange of positions at noon showed we had extended the lead to 300 miles. Aboard both boats it was recognised that the race might depend upon how the South Atlantic high was negotiated, as it was spreading out from Africa to America in our paths and causing light winds over a huge area right down to 38°S. We may have escaped the calms in the doldrums but it looked as if we were about to be plunged into them in a big way, and at this point the battle between the routiers really began to hot up. Somehow we had to break through this area, using all our combined patience and skills accumulated in years of sailing and all the knowledge Bob Rice had tucked away in forty years as a meteorologist.

But at least we embarked on this stage with a surprising 300-mile advantage over *Lyonnaise* who we anticipated would close in during this leg where conditions were expected to favour them. Bob's instructions were quite simple: leave the centre of the high to the east and keep going south. Olivier was already taking a more easterly course, possibly because the temptation to take the shorter route was irresistible or perhaps because he was advised to go that way. It was nail-biting stuff because, although we should, in theory, get the good winds sooner, we knew the high could fragment or move to give him a favourable wind at any time. We would have appreciated more frequent reports of *Lyonnaise*'s position instead of once daily.

However, the initial indications were promising since de Kersuason appeared to be slowing, whereas 200 miles further to the west we retained winds which were showing signs of coming around more from the north, which might be caused by the oceanic circulatory pattern. In fact on the 28th the wind was north-west, an exciting move which could mean that Bob was wrong and the high was moving to enable us to get round to its south. Unfortunately, it did not last, although we used it effectively whilst it was there. The wind soon eased to a force 3 and continued to back, from south-west to south, then south-easterly and then on the 29th it was easterly at force 2. This confirmed what Bob was saying, that the centre remained to the south and we must continue the policy of making southing at all costs. He did relent slightly, however, and allow us to take the easterly bias if there was a choice between east or west of south.

We suffered with very light airs on the 29th and the day's run at noon was the lowest so far, a mere 198 miles, but there was consolation in that *Lyonnaise* dropped back a further twenty miles, so at least she had not discovered a private wind and forged ahead. In the negligible winds the huge mainsail crashed back and forth. In twelve hours we covered only nineteen miles, proof, if any were needed, that even the fastest and lightest of sailing machines cannot move without wind! The battens prevent the mainsail from cracking, but the noise was disturbing for those off watch trying to sleep and a permanent reminder of the lack of progress, even if the mere movement of the sail back and forth produced a speed of up to 1.4 knots. Barry took the opportunity to dive overboard and inspect the port rudder, which had caught on a mooring before we sailed. He reported the only sign of damage was some missing filler in the hull. We could live with that. As he swam across to check the other side I watched him enviously. We were only 33°S and it was hot on deck. To hell with it, I could swim faster than the boat was sailing and there were no clouds in sight which might bring a sudden wind. I stripped and dived in from the bow and had a lovely cool, leisurely swim between the two hulls in the clear blue water. This not only made me feel great, it was by far the easiest method of having a wash.

At noon on the 30th January we had covered only 112 miles in the previous twenty-four hours and this was beginning to make serious inroads into the overall average and bite heavily into the cushion built up over the previous two weeks. *Lyonnaise* gained about fifteen miles in the same period but was three degrees to the east, which, seemingly, put her ahead. But she was closer to the high's centre, which was ominously beginning to move towards the pair of us.

Bob Rice's view was that we were in a very small corridor, perhaps only sixty miles across, where there was slightly more wind than elsewhere and we should continue heading south as our position five degrees further south of *Lyonnaise* could now give a crucial edge. If the high's centre did move towards the two boats we held the superior position and this gap of 300 miles could suddenly be worth three days' sailing or, in good winds, up to 1,200 miles. One does not like to wish a competitor bad luck, especially knowing how frustrating calms are, and anyway I superstitiously believe it likely to bring the bad luck back on one's own head to do so, but we were in a race and anything which slowed *Lyonnaise*, so long as it was not physically damaging, was to our benefit. In any case the matter was outside our control, he was following his routier's advice, we were following ours. It was just reassuring to know that if the high moved south it would delay *Lyonnaise* equally, so we had them covered.

Shortly after lunch a sooty albatross flew past. He was the first Southern Ocean visitor this trip and seemed like a good omen. As if in response, the wind began to go firm. It swung round to the south-west, but for a while it had been swinging everywhere in cat's-paws, so hopes were not raised, but soon it rose slowly and steadily and by nightfall was a steady force 4–5. The sea was flat calm for a while and we flew along on a course east of south, putting distance between us and the high and exulting in our good fortune. When the seas began to increase we eased off ten degrees further from south for a smoother ride. Although the faster we could travel south the better, ten degrees would make little difference and it is doubtful if we actually lost any southing per hour as the speed was higher. The situation could not be better as we were on our favourite point of sailing, a broad reach.

The positions at noon the next day, the 31st, told the story. Now we were seven degrees south of *Lyonnaise* and on the same longitude. We had covered 437 miles in the last twenty-four hours, whereas *Lyonnaise* was stuck, barely making 8 knots to our 18, so the lead was now over 400 miles and growing by the hour. Her course, too, was just south of east, as if they had not noticed the high and were still taking the short cut. Not only were they not escaping from the high, they were steering straight into it and, although a rising southerly sea was now forcing us to steer a course of 130°, we were rapidly escaping from its clutches. The frustration aboard *Lyonnaise* could be imagined only too clearly.

That evening we crossed the 40th parallel in longitude 18°53′ and moved out of the Atlantic, thus completing the first leg of the voyage. Despite the recent calm, it had taken only 15 days, 7 hours and 21 minutes to cover the 5,921 miles from Ushant, an average speed of

16.12 knots and a daily run of 386.84 miles. On the Jules Verne front we were three days ahead of schedule to circumnavigate in seventy-seven days and the gap between *Lyonnaise* and ourselves was widening. Spirits were high as we swept into the roaring forties and the Southern Ocean.

7

Second Chance with the Southern Ocean

The roaring forties have such a reputation for atrocious weather that huge seas and stormy winds are anticipated from the moment a boat crosses the 40th parallel and this can be the case. On my first foray in 1968 I was hit by six gales in ten days but that was in September, still winter in the southern hemisphere. This time we crossed into the Southern Ocean a month after midsummer when conditions are usually more clement, safer and suitable for a high-speed voyage in a lightweight craft. The truth about the weather in the region is that there is a complete range, including calms, but the average wind strength towards the bottom of the world is certainly higher than in any other ocean. On this occasion we were greeted initially by lighter winds and we managed only 298 miles to noon on the 1st February, after sailing more than 400 miles on the 31st January. The cause was the South Atlantic high pressure system again, still edging southwards but swinging to the east towards us, bringing lighter winds in the process. So it was vital to run ahead of it.

But at least we had some speed. Behind us *Lyonnaise* was almost stationary in the centre of the system and achieved only 7 knots on the 2nd and an even worse 4 knots on the 3rd before the combination of the high movement eastwards and their own tortoise-like progress enabled them to crawl sufficiently south to reach the westerlies and get going again. At this point our lead was nearly 1,000 miles and we were maintaining good daily averages of 14–18 knots. A gap such as this meant that effectively we were racing in different stadiums as we were no longer sharing the same weather. This lead was a huge hedge which allowed a little relaxation with, consequently, reduced wear and tear on sails and equipment. Simultaneously, we reckoned it increased the demands on *Lyonnaise* because, if they narrowed the gap, they would eventually rejoin our weather system and with the performances of the boats so equal they would have difficulty overtaking us. At this stage just to catch up they needed to average fifteen miles a day more than us between now and the finish, an average of 0.6 knots. This was a large handicap and of course we might be lucky and have better weather, adding further to the deficit. In general, since the weather would reach them first, they could be expected to speed up as each front arrived and narrow the gap and then, as the front passed, they would slow and we would speed up when it got to us.

But if we regarded the threat from *Lyonnaise* a little more easily, we could not forget the time target to beat, so relaxation was only relative. To achieve a seventy-seven-day circumnavigation we were relying on the Southern Ocean, with its reasonably constant westerly air flow, to allow us to maintain an average of 410 miles a day, just over 17 knots. At this speed we would be in the roaring forties for twenty-eight days between Tristan da Cunha and Cape Horn. As on the previous voyage, we anticipated sailing the first half of the Southern Ocean, about as far as Australia, at about 40°S, but in response to Bob Rice's advice we dived south as far as 45°30′ by the 3rd in order to put more space between ourselves and the high. On the 4th we eased a little north but immediately received a typically colloquial warning to "Keep out of the gutters, particularly the left-hand one." Bob's 'road' extended between 43°–46°S. To the north of this would lie calms, to the south stronger winds which created larger seas and, although we might crash along at 25 knots for a while, these would oblige us to throttle back and the end result would be a slower average overall. From the outset of the adventure Bob was personally and enthusiastically involved to the extent that he stopped shaving when we crossed the start line at Ushant and now he was becoming 'a little gamey', as he put it but, superstitiously, felt he dare not shave – he called it his contribution!

The circumference of the earth at 50°S, the middle latitude of the Southern Ocean, is nearly 14,000 miles and on average it is 1,200 miles wide. Throughout the ocean there is a scattering of small islands, many, but not all, discovered by Captain James Cook during his voyages in search of a southern continent. None was inhabited when first found and there was no civilisation or craft capable of colonising anything in this ocean before the arrival of the Europeans. Today some are host to small parties of scientists and only the Falklands and Tristan da Cunha have permanent resident populations, all of European extraction. Tristan da Cunha was discovered by a Portuguese of that name in the early part of the sixteenth century. We passed well to the south, and were also ninety miles south of its nearest neighbour, Gough Island, which is home to seven South African meteorologists who overheard us calling Cape Town radio station and asked them to put us in contact. The reason was soon apparent. Their spell of duty is almost a year, the winters are cold and bitter and in the summers the main vegetation is seven-foot-high ferns which makes a casual walk a major expedition. Our contact sounded desperate to have a conversation with someone new. It cannot be an easy posting and they deserved a medal for the job, as they provided one of the very few sources of accurate meteorological data in the whole ocean. Unfortunately, we were travelling fast and could not always afford the loss of sleep to keep a radio schedule on a regular basis.

As the godpod also served as the radio room, this created a problem for the person off watch and trying to sleep. I usually had no difficulty sleeping through the sound of voices when Peter was operating the radio, but he was a lighter sleeper and would always wake if I was using it. So I tried to arrange schedules that missed his rest time. This was not always easy to predict as we switched our watches around and we also altered the ship's clock as we travelled east so we kept times which were relevant to daily routines. If this had not been done we would have had breakfast at 8 am on longitude 0°, at noon at longitude 60°, 4 pm at 120° and 8 pm at 180°. Since most people are programmed to have meals at roughly morning, midday and evening, we changed the clocks to coincide with the movement of the sun but always had one clock going on GMT, or Universal Coordinated Time as the French and Americans now insist on calling it, as this is the basis for navigation and radio schedules.

There was one exception to my rule about Peter's sleep and that was the weekly schedule with Peter Dunning and the other hams in the USA. Each week we attempted to reach each other, our success varying with times and distances. On balance we had good communications on 12 and 16 megahertz in the Atlantic, but they were less reliable down south. I could usually hear Fred, whose call sign was KWS578, from Fall River, Mass., even when the others were unreadably weak, but he did have the most power and best antenna arrangements.

As we plunged further south the temperature fell and urgent calls for all hands became very unpopular, since this implied an emergency and people had to come on deck without time to get into protective clothing. A gybe, and there were plenty of them at this stage as we zigzagged between Bob Rice's limits, could usually be planned and sufficient notice given to allow people to dress properly in waterproof clothing. We were not racing round buoys and it was unimportant if we continued on one gybe a little longer when both were equidistant from the rhumb line and there were thousands of miles to the nearest land. On the 5th, however, Peter gave a few of us a soaking when we were all called for a gybe that suddenly could not wait to allow people to get ready. To make matters worse I had just put away my dirty washing, had a fresh-water rinse and made a complete change into clean clothes. This was the unnecessary price of impatience, but after the batten-breaking incident in the previous voyage nobody was prepared to take chances when gybing. I snuggled back into the warmth of a well-padded sleeping bag as quickly as possible after the gybe was complete. It might become more damp from contact with the wet clothes, but it always warmed up after a while from body heat.

On the 5th we celebrated the third day in a row with a day's run above 400 miles. We were beginning to boost our average once more after the delays in the high. We also passed through the longitude of Cape Town. It had taken 19 days, 17 hours and 53 minutes from the start line at Ushant, a full 1 day, 18 hours and 55 minutes faster than *Commodore* and the previous world record. Our time from the equator to this position, however, was 12 days, 13 hours and 29 minutes, which does leave room for improvement. We were 43°S at noon, which was 500 miles south of Cape Point. If we had taken a more northerly course the distance would be less to Cape Town and therefore a faster time, however we were shaping a course for Australia which gave us a good separation from the Agulhas Bank.

The same afternoon Steve Anscell reappeared, this time in a South African C-130 Hercules aircraft from 27 Squadron who were now old friends after their contact during the previous voyage. They flew out over the ocean from Cape Town and found our tiny boat, a pinprick in this vast area, with ease. Once again they circled patiently whilst the film was radioed to them and then treated us to a magnificent low-level fly past as they departed. Steve seemed more relaxed than usual, one sensed he felt a good deal safer with this airline than in some of his earlier transport!

We were now 1,600 miles ahead of schedule for a seventy-seven-day rounding and when we obtained *Lyonnaise*'s position on the 6th the lead was 970 miles. They were at last in the Southern Ocean at 42°S and making good headway but not closing the gap. We were aware that Olivier disliked announcing bad news, so on the days we heard nothing from him we assumed he was not doing well and were usually proved right. This consistency of behaviour was rather self-defeating and if he really wanted to scare us he would have kept quiet when he was going well rather than the other way round. Then his silences would have made us look nervously over our shoulders. It would also have created more excitement amongst the journalists. When we looked at the forecast it appeared we had a good week of south-westerly winds of between 25–30 knots on the way with the stronger winds at the beginning, whereas *Lyonnaise*'s forecast looked to be lighter over the same period. If this were the case, we were almost certainly in for a period of silence from our competitor.

These forecasts proved partially correct. On the 7th, as we passed 120 miles north of the South African research station at Marion Island, we were dodging squalls of gale force and going like a train. Our day's run was 478 miles, which put sixty-eight miles in the bank. There was water everywhere, flung up by the bows and occasionally thrown into the cockpit by waves bouncing off the inside of the hulls. The cockpit was dryer now with the changes to the hulls but that was relative, it was still a place that called for full oilskins. Bucketing around like this made the motion awkward and it was hard to move about without a handhold. No one was sleeping very well as the noise and vibration made people restless. It is hard to describe the noise exactly, but despite the modifications we had made in two major refits it was still like being in an underground train charging over points at speed with a dozen high pressure water hoses playing on it. In the godpod there was the additional effect of waves crashing into the floor with a terrifying cracking noise which made you fear the whole thing was going to disintegrate at any moment, that is after gravity returned one to the bunk, because each of the blows tossed us into the air! As Peter and I attempted to lie in our bunks we were constantly calling to the man on the wheel to ease up and watch for the big ones or reduce sail if necessary. Then once we were on deck, where both the noise and vibration were less obvious, we were pushing the boat along as hard as anyone. You need to be a joint skipper to appreciate fully just how annoying this must appear to the rest of the crew – constantly bollocked for doing something the skipper does not realise he is doing himself!

It was incredible sailing though, and steering was really fun. The trick was to bring the boat round, away from straight downwind, until the sails began to work efficiently as an aerofoil and then, as the boat accelerated and brought the wind forward, bear away because the boat's speed was augmenting the wind speed. Combining this with being just in front of a wave led to some wonderful surfing bursts of speed, the highest on this occasion being 29.7 knots. However, we were always a little cautious about these figures because the instruments are designed to work in water and when we were travelling in this manner there was a lot of aeration along the surface of the hulls and nothing could be totally relied upon. We knew it was fast but could not be certain exactly how fast. All one could say with certainty was that if the spinnaker was still set it was time it came down!

Angus was learning high-speed, big-wave sailing in a giant multihull very quickly. When we first entered the Southern Ocean he was misled by the moderate conditions and commented disdainfully that he didn't think the waves very impressive. Now, with winds of gale to storm force and waves to suit, he was becoming more respectful. He was a little nervous of steering the first time it was his turn in the high seas, which pleased me as it showed he was taking them seriously. A big wave is awesome. A small hill moving at more than 30 knots, sometimes with a breaking crest, is always impressive and potentially dangerous, and I would rather put my life in the hands of someone who treats them with caution. On *Condor* in the 1977 Whitbread we had to restrict steering in gales to five experienced helmsmen at the start of the first Southern Ocean leg because the others just could not cope. Fortunately, they all could by the finish, which spread the workload. *Enza*, with twin rudders, was far more responsive than *Condor* and it was hours rather than days before Angus was left to steer for his full hour trick. Rudders are like brakes, the more they are applied the more they slow the boat. Ideally, they should be kept amidships and the boat balanced with her sails to maintain a straight course. This is seldom possible in sheltered waters and out of the question in large seas, but the good helmsman is the person who uses the helm least to maintain course because more ground will be covered.

On the 8th February we were passing north of the Crozet Islands, a French territory and occasionally inhabited. Some kelp, very thick and long brown seaweed which is normally a sign of land since it attaches itself to rocks on the sea bottom, gave us a worry but it was weed which had broken loose from its anchorage and not a hitherto undiscovered shoal. During the last thirty or so years a number of sea-mounts have been discovered in the Southern Ocean which lie closer to the surface than was realised, some still growing through volcanic action. It is necessary to bear in mind that charts can only show information from sectors which have been checked. As traffic in the Southern Ocean is light, it is not so well surveyed as the other oceans, so there is always the slight chance one might meet an unexpected shoal. That evening Peter opened a large heavy package left aboard by his daughter which turned out to contain a four-foot-high inflatable penguin. He nearly expired blowing it up and when fully inflated it filled half the pod. The sight was so improbable we collapsed into hysterical laughter, as in the dim light of the godpod it looked so realistic. Eventually, one of the watch on deck poked his nose round the screen at the entrance to find out what was so funny and the look of astonishment on his face at seeing three occupants of the cabin set us off again.

The rather unpleasant squalls and seas continued and we began to

wonder whether they were due to an unusually high sea-water
temperature. This varied quite a lot, like the Gulf Stream, and the
readings were between 14°–18°C, the latter being the temperature that
day off Bermuda according to Bob Rice, yet here we were at 43°S.
There had to be a logical explanation, perhaps an eddy from the
Indian Ocean or a continuation of the Agulhas current, but we were at
52°E and thought it surprising that warm water extended this far. Not
that we were complaining, since the water slopping into the cockpit
was not so chilly and the temperature in the hulls remained reasonably
warm.

The weather did not improve, indeed there was a gust of 48 knots of
wind the following night which combined with a cross sea of waves
from the south-west and north-west to make life miserable. We
considered heading more to the north to seek calmer waters but
decided against as we were holding our own and there was quieter
weather on the way from the west. So we reduced sail steadily until we
were down to a fully reefed mainsail and nothing else. This had little
effect on speed but the boat felt less pressed, which made her safer, as
we had greater control. Too much sail had produced too much power
and the helmsman was working overtime to hold the course and
finding it increasingly difficult to check any yaws which were threatening as the waves grew dangerously to about fifty feet in height.
From now on the boat was held down wave to keep the sterns to the
waves. If we swung round the waves would have crashed into the
larger surface of the hull sides and jerked the boat off course, which
was inviting serious trouble. In spite of all precautions we were still
surfing down the front of some waves and, when this rush coincided
with a gust, we were in danger of catching the wave ahead.

Sure enough before long we fell back from the crest of one wave
which just failed to carry us along with it and were immediately picked
up by the forward slope of the next one, which was following more
quickly than normal. This phenomenon happens occasionally and in
the case of tightly packed waves, usually steeper than the others
because of their compression, it seemed to arrive in threes every ten
minutes or so. We began to accelerate forward with Angus holding the
head straight down wave. Soon we were moving as fast as the wave
and then we roared ahead as gravity and wind combined. In front was

the steep back of the wave which had just overtaken us. I watched as we shot towards it, wondering whether the bows would rise and lift over its top. We hurtled closer, there was nothing we could do but steer straight and avoid a broach. The bows dug into the wave, the downward force was too great for the reserves of buoyancy and they disappeared beneath the surface. The effect was like running into a brick wall and the boat came to an immediate full stop. 'Falling down the mine' was the way the crew described it.

Angus was thrown forward on the wheel, I was beside him and was flung against the back end of the coach roof but, fortunately, my hands were free and so I was able to cushion the force of the blow. The boat gave the impression of being vertical, indeed there was a danger that, with the bows held by the sea and the sterns free, we could have pitchpoled, or done a somersault. When I glanced behind to check Angus was still on the helm, I could see both rudders suspended eight to ten feet above the water. The boat was totally out of control for that short moment, we had to rely upon the science of ship design to bring her down into the sea and back on an even keel. It always seems an age and time slows down in such circumstances, but then as the wave passed beneath us, the sail once more exerted greater force than the sea and we charged off again. In the hulls the off watch crews were thrown into a tangle of bodies, sleeping bags and clothing at the front end of the compartments and in the godpod Peter, who was just coming out on deck, lost his grip around the entrance and cannoned eight feet backwards into the chart table. The breath was knocked out of him but, far worse, when he tried to move there was a sharp pain in his back.

I poked my head into the godpod and saw Peter at the fore end breathing shallowly to reduce the pain. His ribs hurt badly and he thought some might be broken or cracked. I relieved Angus on the helm and sent him in to investigate. He was unable to say if anything was broken, the bruises had still to form, but the initial diagnosis was that two or three could be cracked. Angus helped Peter undress and got him into his bunk, then put a call through to Hamble to seek advice from Doctor Mark Thomson, who prescribed strong painkillers. Angus had not yet administered these, as he had been warned of their strength, but Tommo assured him they were also an excellent hangover cure! The patient was confined to his bunk for rest and observation. Internal bleeding was the greatest fear but fortunately it never materialised. Angus came in for some leg-pulling because, although he could have done nothing to prevent the accident, he had been steering and was inevitably accused of trying to create patients! But we were all aware of the seriousness of the situation – Peter might or might not be badly hurt but, since we were well beyond the range of helicopters, we would have to divert and put him ashore for hospital treatment if the injuries proved serious.

Whilst we awaited developments we rearranged the watch-keeping system to a seven-man three hours on and four off duty rota, grateful for having been a crew of eight. We could manage with one crew sick, whereas if *Lyonnaise* lost a hand the hours of work would have risen a minimum of twenty-five per cent and really contributed to tiredness and decreased efficiency. So we tucked Peter into his bunk where he was relatively safe. Meals were carried across the trampoline to him in the godpod and the old bucket was brought into service as a WC. We put a call through to Pippa so she would know the exact situation, included the accident in the next report, and pressed on.

Shortly afterwards, ironically, the seas began to ease. Two hours later we let out a reef, and a steady force 5 from the west for the rest of the day allowed the waves to abate sufficiently for another to come out the next morning. Despite our recent drama and the need to proceed with care, we averaged over 400 miles in twenty-four hours for the sixth day in succession. *Lyonnaise* continued to fall back and we now had a lead of 1,425 miles. In desperation they had gone south to increase the likelihood of strong winds and also to reduce the distance to travel. We were at latitude 44°S, they at 48°. This meant that for every sixty miles we each sailed they moved through ninety minutes of longitude to our eighty-four. But the price to pay for this corner cutting was in the chance of extreme weather. The wave sizes at the time of Peter's injury easily persuaded us to remain where we could maintain a high average speed in relative safety.

Peter was not an easy patient. Initially he was in quite a lot of pain and convinced he had cracked ribs, though Mark Thomson's long-distance diagnosis was severe bruising. Sleep and rest were the best cure, but it is hard to sleep well when the bunk keeps shaking, so we brought over one of the mattresses from the port hull to pad out his bunk, and Angus, George and Ed had to 'hot bunk' temporarily. Though more comfortable, our patient remained crotchety. For a while he busied himself concentrating on America's Cup business which kept the generators humming as signal after signal wafted its way to Auckland, but when this subject was exhausted he turned to our progress. He could see the instruments over the chart table showing boat speed, wind speed, wind direction and position but nothing else, so he could only imagine the situation on deck. First he complained the course was wrong and that we were not going fast enough and then, contradictorily, that the boat was going too fast and taking too much of a bashing which would break her up! After a succession of particularly heavy bangs whilst Ed was steering, he suddenly yelled out that if we went on like this, he would never recover and we would have to go to Fremantle to put him in hospital. Sotto voce came a reply from Ed at the helm: "If you go on like this we'll divert especially to put you ashore in Fremantle."

Despite the loss of one person on deck, speed did not suffer and, if *Lyonnaise* had entertained hopes that the accident might cause us to slow, they were doomed to disappointment. As the days passed we maintained a headlong progression of day's runs in excess of 400 miles. In his bunk Peter's bruising went through the phases of red, blue and black and then subsided. Massage was proposed to aid recovery and performed by Barry and Angus in turn. Barry had done a week's course on the subject and his iron fingers seemed tireless. We were all immensely encouraged by Angus's competence when, on his first attempt, he announced, "There is a right way and a wrong way of doing this. I think I'm doing it right!" The down side to all this good work was that the embrocation they employed made the inside of the godpod smell like a boxing gymnasium. It may also have had hallucinogenic properties because George, whose editing studio was in the pod, began to have strange dreams. He dreamed that Peter had been demoted and banished to the starboard hull. His replacement was Jaws, who moved into Peter's bunk in the godpod, donned a red and yellow Hawaiian shirt, put on sun-glasses and read cookery books. Whenever anyone went in to discuss progress or ask for instructions, Jaws tore a page from the cookery book, and gave it to the questioner with instructions to go and create that recipe!

We tip-toed past the position where we came to grief on the first voyage, subconsciously holding our breath, but this time everything was holding together well, despite Peter's fears, as we jumped from wave to wave. We had breakages, of course, sails being the main victim of the headlong rush and involving everyone, even George, in some sewing. George was beavering away, stitching the head of one of the spinnakers back on to the main body, when he announced he might take up a career as a sailmaker when he got home. I looked across at his well-intentioned but nevertheless large, undisciplined stitches. Homeward bounders we call them, as they are only designed to get the ship home and not to last. I suggested he keep his job as a camera-man open!

Nearly all the sail repairs were to spinnakers and not just because, being lightweight, they tore more easily than the other sails but because the equipment used to set them was also very vulnerable. A spinnaker full of wind exerts a huge pull and is very hard to hoist or take down, so all ours were in socks, basically nylon tubes, which enabled them to be hoisted easily and prevented them breaking out before we were ready, but the socks were too fragile and kept tearing. The spinnaker halyards also chafed through, despite attention every hour or so to shift the wear point, and each time this happened the sail fell down, usually into the water, and we were lucky to escape without a tear somewhere. More surprisingly, the clips holding the sail to the halyard, although officially rated at 25,000 pounds strain, sheared on a number of occasions and also dumped the sails.

People are always asking what sailors actually do at sea when not steering. Never-ending maintenance is the answer. Constant vibration means that anything which screws tight has to be checked on a regular basis since it almost inevitably shakes loose after a while. Shackles needed to be moused, or seized with wire, if not routinely tightened, and even solid items like the radio aerial came loose as its locking screws worked free. Replacing this was not an easy job in a big sea. The whole forty-foot-long section had to be unbolted from the deck and the hole covered immediately with a temporary patch to stop water going on to the generator below. Then the unwieldy object was carefully lowered to the deck, with strong wind gusts not helping,

Above left, Angus and George eating on deck to avoid the heat of the galley. Above right, Jaws had a method of short-circuiting the washing up. Below, working on deck, waiting for the next squall in the South Atlantic.

Crossing from hull to godpod could be a wet business (below) in heavy weather, but David has an easier ride bringing tea to the cockpit crew.

Above, the mainsail was set for most of the voyage, so all hands took advantage of a calm day to lower it for necessary maintenance. Below, getting ready for a sail change. We usually called all hands to speed the task.

The big bergs were majestic and easy to see, though we had never intended going far enough south to get among them. It was the growlers we couldn't see that could cause the problems.

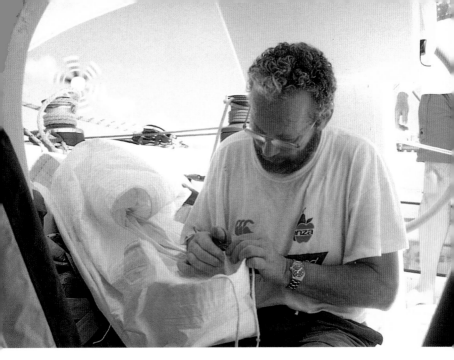

Return to the heat of the South Atlantic brought on some mad hatting. The finished article was no threat to the millinery business but did the job and will last for years.

A really ugly confused sea as we approach the finish line.

Above, this was all the welcome party on the French destroyer could see of us most of the time. Below, sprinting for the line with just the storm jib set and full warps out to prevent us rushing down the waves.

Fresh food at last, the crew celebrates with apples and champagne
at the finish.

tightened up, taped for security and replaced. It required all hands to complete the job.

Another constant source of trouble was the headstay furler, whose grub screws kept shaking loose, so that the sections came apart. When this occurred the sail tore by the gap, which was a difficult repair as the stitching had to be sufficiently small to allow the mended sail to slide into the luff groove. We thought we had bought the Rolls-Royce of furling apparatus but were sadly disillusioned. However, the most ambitious repair was to the bottom of the godpod where the constant pounding created cracks at the edges which we discovered when salt water collected in the V at the bottom even when people were not moving in and out in wet oilskins. Barry cut up some of the light-weight floorboards from the hull storage areas and shaped them to make floors which fitted right across the vulnerable part and then used epoxy and glass tape to stick them in place. He made a first-class job, so the bottom no longer gave slightly as each wave struck, though it meant the shock seemed to focus on the seats and bunks once more. I'm not sure which was the more uncomfortable sensation, but the reinforcements gave a greater feeling of security.

Some of the other work undertaken was also quite sophisticated. For example, the spinnaker head block box in the mast was very slightly out of true, with the result that the carbon fibre at its front edge was eventually ground down and the sheaves jammed. Ed and Barry removed it, setting up a temporary rig so we could still set a spinnaker, and Barry disappeared into the microscopic workshop to organise a repair. His first attempt was interrupted by someone leaping down to get something and kicking the box before it had set, so he had to start all over again. Perseverance paid off in the end and the box was replaced after a few days and restored normal service.

The Kerguelen Islands passed south on the 10th, yet another smoking day with a run over 400 miles. This is a fascinating group, owned by France, which maintains a small scientific community, plus volunteers who can elect to do their military service here and gain remission of time because of the harsh conditions. The main settle-ment is typically French according to David, who stopped there once for repairs. In the 1840s the islands were a huge whaling and sealing base and when whaling eventually died out, they were leased to two gentlemen who tried sealing and sheep-breeding with varying success. The Germans used the islands, which were by then uninhabited, as a base for commerce raiders during the Second World War. The chart makes the group look a perfect cruising ground but the average wind strength would suggest that very heavy ground tackle of anchor and chain would be advisable.

A few weeks before we passed, the British Whitbread competitor *Dolphin and Youth* had called in to fix her rudder as this is allowed under those rules. We were not quite sure where we stood in similar circumstances; if we were to go in for repairs and someone gave us the parts we needed, we assumed it counted as outside assistance, but what if we went ashore and bought the same parts from a store; would beaching the boat and something simple like a helper placing a rubber tyre beneath the hull also count as outside assistance? The Jules Verne rules could do with some fine turning on these points. *Lyonnaise*, of course, was cocking a Gallic snook at them and Olivier had made it clear he would go into harbour if he needed to. It was a topic for endless speculation. On the boat there was no camp fire to sit around for such discussions, time in cabins was usually spent sleeping or at least being quiet so as to leave others undisturbed. Apart from brief encounters at meals, the cockpit provided the only place where we could talk, but even then the helmsman was left out as he had to concentrate. So in our case conversation was usually limited to just two people.

Our high speed was crashing us through longitude eastwards and covering ten degrees with 400 plus miles each day in latitude. Behind us *Lyonnaise* was hanging on, the gap was 1,424 miles on the 10th, 1,293 on the 12th, 1,280 on the 13th, 1,433 on the 14th, 1,362 on the 15th, as we each underwent different conditions. They were still well south with Olivier making much of his bravery in taking such a dangerous track. He announced to the world that he was waiting for us to break up, but he was the one in the more vulnerable latitude. His morale was still high, however, and he claimed a new world record for a twenty-four-hour run of 524 miles which could not later be recognised as he lacked the independent position-fixing equipment on board.

On the 12th we were treated to the first of what became a regular fantastic display of the Aurora Australis. Great laser beams of light flashed up from the horizon to the south and puffs of white illuminated sky swept above us at speeds far greater than the wind. It was awesome and primaeval, made more impressive by the absence of the moon, and one could imagine how our ancestors might have imagined it to stem from an angry god. The cause has a perfectly satisfactory scientific explanation – electrically charged particles emanating from the sun at a time of increased sun spot activity are directed by the earth's magnetic field towards the two magnetic poles. When they strike atmospheric gases, sixty or so miles above the earth's surface, they induce them to light up in this spectacular fashion, and what we could see were very strong displays of rays and rayed bands and arcs. It was the strength of the performance which was surprising as 53°S is usually the lowest latitude for such a show, a good 600 miles away. It was extraordinarily beautiful and I have never seen its like, even well into the Arctic Circle.

Rainbows were common, too, and we often saw both ends. George rushed up, camera in hand, to film one, saying as he did so, "You can tell a lot about a person by their reaction to a rainbow." This had to be challenged, of course, and I asked him what on earth he was talking about. He responded that the love of a rainbow showed a love of simple things. From his bunk in the godpod Peter's recuperating voice rang out, "Oh, that must explain why we like you then, George?"

When the longitude of Cape Leeuwin, the south-western cape of Australia, zipped past shortly after noon on the 15th February we were 29 days, 16 hours from Ushant. It had taken only 9 days, 22 hours to cover the distance from Cape Point, South Africa, representing eighty-seven degrees of longitude, or 3,765 miles, a quarter of the way around the world. However, progress was about to slow as we could not avoid a large high pressure system working its way southward into the Great Australian Bight and bringing lighter winds. This was the first day after eleven when the day's run did not exceed 400 miles, so to obtain stronger winds, we started to trek south to retain the fast conditions whilst we waited for another front which arrived after nightfall, forcing us to reduce sail to a two-reefed mainsail and the staysail.

During the day in the easier conditions Peter had emerged from the pod and taken the helm for a short while, but found he could not yet stand for long. We had hoped that this might be the beginning of a return to normal duties, but obviously it was too soon. He retreated to his bunk again and the service from meals on keels continued. Later in the day we made contact with Mike Golding aboard *Group 4* who had just passed Tasmania coming from the other direction in his attempt at the east to west record for a solo non-stop circumnavigation against winds and currents. The old record dated back to 1970 when it was set by Chay Blyth, so a challenge was long overdue. Mike sounded in good fettle and was well ahead of schedule. He told me he was looking at a time of 180 days but since he was going so well I could not see why he wasn't pushing for something faster. Days in hand in record attempts are like money in the bank, hard to collect and very easily dissipated, it only requires a small breakage to halve the speed and the bank is suddenly emptied. He eventually succeeded in his quest and produced a new record for an east to west circumnavigation of 161 days, 17 hours, 35 minutes, 30 seconds from the same Ushant to Lizard line we were using.

This was my day for a wash and change of clothing. The moment had to be chosen carefully since a warmer day made the process more bearable and, as it was almost two weeks since I last cleaned up properly, I decided the time was right for me. We all had special thermal underclothing and I had brought along four sets of long johns and sweat shirts, intending to make two changes in the Southern Ocean. In these latitudes it was not an evolution to be performed on deck, the WC compartment was the chosen location, simply because it had a heater. The secret was to switch on the heater early to allow the compartment to warm up, then zip up the curtain, not for modesty, but to retain the heat. Some people ferried warm water across from the galley in a saucepan or kettle, a hazardous journey on the course of which most was lost and what remained cooled with spray. I did not bother with this and regretted it as the fresh water in the storage container was close to freezing. There was a small basin which I filled, soaked the sponge, rubbed on soap, gritted my teeth and applied to the skin, but the shock was so horrible that I held the next spongeful in a blast of warm air from the heater. It was only a slight improvement. This was one of those chores it would be nice to avoid but now it was started, the sooner finished the better. Water, of course, went flying everywhere and redressing without wetting the fresh clothing was almost impossible with the boat lurching around. Feeling clean and superior I made my way back to the cockpit, biding my time before committing the rush across the trampoline where a rogue wave could so easily have spoiled all the good work. Trampoline crossings were a great game. No one at the helm deliberately tried to soak another crew member, indeed we usually bore off to make the crossing less risky, but to date I had managed better than most to avoid being dowsed and I knew it would cause merriment if I was caught. It was as well I had my ablutions when I did, as two days later Ed switched on the heater without connecting its exhaust to the hull outlet. The immediate result was the near asphyxiation of the off-watch inhabitants of the starboard hull, followed shortly afterwards by the collapse of the fan motor. So drying out clothes and washing in the warm became history until we moved into milder climes again, which would not be before we were well past Cape Horn.

The front we were awaiting gave a run of 459 miles the next day and 456 the following one, superb powerboat stuff that we were confident of sustaining almost indefinitely, as we were travelling east at almost the same rate as the front, so the seas did not build up, which was of tremendous assistance. Further back, though, where the system had matured, life was nothing like so happy for *Lyonnaise*.

On the 17th February we passed south of the Spencer Gulf where most of the grain ships loaded right up until the last proper grain race in 1939. It was interesting to compare our speed with that of the square-riggers a century earlier. It took us thirty-two and a half days to pass this longitude from Ushant. The best time I can trace for the great *Herzogin Cecilie* (typical of the vessels built towards the end of the era of sail) is sixty-seven days, which was considered very good when ninety days was the average. The record for square-rig at fifty-nine days (nearly double our time) was held by *Thermopylae*, which had been built for speed on the tea trade. We were therefore averaging twice the speed of the best and three times the speed of the average commercial sailing ships with acres of sail but heavy displacements.

South of New Zealand the variation of the earth's magnetic field (which is what the compass needle follows) reaches forty-five degrees, which meant the compass was giving a reading forty-five degrees away from true. Unfortunately, our electronic compasses could not be adjusted beyond thirty degrees, so could not be compensated enough to make them read accurately. The increased variation also meant the directive force for the steering compass was so reduced that it became less 'dead beat' and swung a lot, making it less reliable. In order to have a better reference for the course to steer, we therefore relied upon the course-over-ground reading from the GPS. It was not perfect, since it was much harder to anticipate the swings of the boat, the real secret of steering a good course, but it did enable us to steer a reasonable one.

As we pressed on towards New Zealand a high formed just to the north at about 42°S/155°E and began to move east. Over New Zealand there was a developing depression which would normally slide south and allow the high to move north of it, the usual pattern formed across the Pacific Ocean, but, unfortunately, this one was to be the exception. The high was due to extend into an east/west-lying ridge which would pass south of the low, and this combination would create an easterly air stream in the roaring forties. Bob Rice was concerned that such an upset to the normal pattern might take time to sort out and if we were to achieve good speeds or even just maintain sufficient to be ahead of the record schedule it was essential to retain the westerly winds. We were somewhat taken aback however when he instructed us to go to 60°S, as this placed us well into the iceberg area and it was never planned to hazard our lightweight boat in icy seas. There is an old sailor's adage:

> Beyond 40° south there is no law.
> Beyond 50° south there is no God.

They did not come up with anything for 'Beyond 60° south' – it was probably beyond imagination. But whatever happened, any involvement with the low, which might well move south-east, was out of the question. The alternative was to head north and perhaps pass through the Cook Strait between North and South Island of New Zealand, a rather extreme course of action, but one which would keep us on the right side of the low. Confirmation of Bob's prognosis came with a more westerly air stream, a steady barometer and, as a bonus, an easing sea.

The choices were stark: stay at the planned latitude and run into easterlies and come to a stop; go north above the low, through the Cook Strait and follow the low south when it moved; or dive south, as Bob was suggesting, and stay below a rather unreliable-looking ridge of high pressure which might suddenly disappear leaving us at the mercy of the descending low and easterlies. We could be forgiven for feeling frustrated, since this weather pattern seemed designed to thwart us, whilst *Lyonnaise* was too far away to be affected by it and was being given a wonderful opportunity to catch up. The success of the whole project might rest on our making the right choice. If we made the wrong one we could lose any hope of the record. A three-way conversation with Bob eventually concluded the southerly option was the least risky, largely because it involved the smallest diversion, so, conscious of what was at stake, we explained the problem and our conclusions to the rest of the crew and headed south.

This allowed *Lyonnaise* to narrow the gap somewhat since we were no longer sailing exactly away from her, something many people ashore again did not appreciate and, indeed, the initial reaction from our PR supporters was a mild panic that *Lyonnaise* was closing in. Since the day's runs dropped only slightly below 400 miles per day, it should have been apparent that other factors were at work, but not everyone is good at geometry! From our point of view we were far more absorbed monitoring the developing weather and the falling barometer as our latitude increased and searching out extra clothing as the air and sea-water temperatures dropped.

On the 19th, ten days after his accident, Peter felt well enough to rejoin the watch-keeping system. He still had twinges and was certainly not a hundred per cent fit but psychologically he needed to return to the deck and feel fully part of the team again. Although we had managed very well without him, it was good to have the whole crew working together and, as a bonus, to enjoy an extra hour's sleep as the time off watch returned to five hours from four. We nearly had to revert to the shortened system the following day when Jaws suddenly collapsed in the cockpit. We never did identify the exact cause, he just suddenly lost all his energy. 'Doctor' Angus diagnosed a

dietary deficiency and took appropriate steps. Prescribing food for
Jaws was rather like administering alcohol to a drunk, but it did the
trick, and the symptons did not recur.

Our busy, but private world was briefly invaded on the 21st when a
P-3 Orion aircraft of the Royal New Zealand Air Force overflew us
whilst on a routine fishery patrol. They circled whilst we sent up the
latest film, which enabled us to update everyone. New Zealand was
currently having a surfeit of sailing as the Whitbread Race had just
restarted and this fleet was slightly ahead and north of us but bound
for the same immediate destination, Cape Horn.

New Zealand was the halfway mark and we reached it in under
thirty-six days, a faster time than anticipated. Despite gaining in the
last few days, *Lyonnaise* was still over 800 miles astern, a formidable
distance which would take her at least two days to cover if we just
stayed put and we had no such intentions. As far as the Jules Verne
Trophy was concerned we were running more than six days ahead of
schedule. Bob Rice had guided us magnificently through or round
every meteorological obstacle with hardly a pause. We had been
incredibly lucky so far – but the abnormal weather continued to
put everything at risk.

8

Our Luck Turns

The depression over New Zealand deepened and created unexpected hail storms which destroyed a third of the ripening fruit crop, leaving many of the growers we had met during the tour with the boat only four months ago facing serious hardship, some even bankruptcy, and here we were spending their money to break a world record. We felt desperately sorry for them but knew we were helping them in the only way we could. The apple business could only recover if the remainder of the harvest fetched good prices and marketing, for which we were literally the flagship, was an important factor in this.

Having wreaked havoc in New Zealand, the depression moved south-east and weakened slightly but the easterly winds associated with its southern perimeter spread out in front of us to cover an immense area of ocean to 55°S. Effectively it was doing what Bob had said it would, creating easterly winds where westerlies were the norm, a complete reversal of the usual weather pattern. Having been forced south by this aberration we did find force 5 westerly winds along the 60th parallel but between us and the easterly winds to the north lay a long band of calms. To go a hundred miles north would mean sitting still in calms and beyond them only a further hundred miles would lie the easterlies which entailed beating into headwinds. These were both recipes for disaster and in order to remain on target there was no choice but to stay south for the present. Even here we had to be vigilant as Bob Rice was predicting a small bubble of high pressure might develop ahead at 63°S and 175°W within a day. On the 21st February we were 540 miles from that position, possibly a day and a

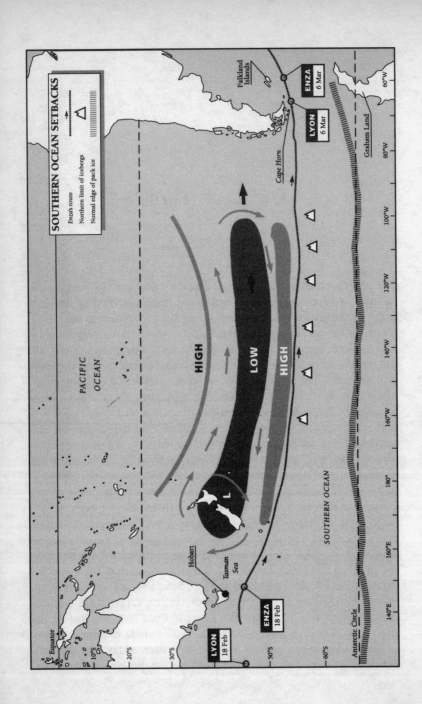

half away. We prayed that Bob was wrong or this system delayed.

There was one small compensation. At 170°E we were 120 degrees of longitude from Cape Horn and at 60°S this was a distance of only 3,600 miles. But the price to pay for this advantage was the danger of being within 200 miles of the mean limit of the pack ice, the solid crust of ice which surrounds the Antarctic continent. Huge chunks are constantly broken off to begin a drift north-eastwards into the Southern Ocean where they fragment and melt. Icebergs of fifty or more miles in length, small uncharted islands, present a hazard to the largest of vessels and for us to strike one could be fatal. However the large bergs are less of a menace in these days of radar than that posed by growlers, small lumps that splinter off from the main bergs and lie, just showing on the surface, but difficult to spot. At this far south, too, if a new depression did come through near the usual path, we would be near to the centre with its attendant high winds and freezing conditions, which did not bear thinking about.

As we moved south the radar was switched on and a lookout posted forward for half-hour spells only, as the cold penetrated right through oilskins. Although the wind dropped to force 4–5, we were still achieving more than 400 miles each day at this stage, which gave it quite a high chill factor. The sea-water temperature fell to 2°C and everything felt cold, although the air was dry enough to hang out clothing to freeze dry as one joker put it!

As Magellan's crew were the first to discover, if you sail around the world you find yourself one day behind if you go westabout and one day ahead if eastabout when you return to your starting point. Sailing eastwards across the International Date Line we jumped back one day in a micro-second or, put another way, we were just beginning Tuesday with New Zealand and immediately went back to the beginning of Monday. If this is confusing, spare a thought for the survivors of Magellan's crew who had to explain why they were on a different day when they arrived home!

Lines drawn on a chart to indicate varying degrees of ice density are, of necessity, bound to be theoretical, but once across the International Date Line we were officially into a zone where icebergs could be expected in a density of one to every forty-five miles of ocean. So it was not too much of a shock when at tea time on the 22nd we saw the first, a very large berg which we could see at eleven miles and which radar picked up at nine miles. The range was not fantastic, especially as the object was so large, but good enough for safety. The whole crew tumbled out to watch, as there is a grand beauty about icebergs which never pales, however many you may have seen before.

Behind us *Lyonnaise* started to drop south as well, but whilst we were at the eastern end of the high and travelling along with it, she was at the west and benefiting from a slight diminution in size of the system. On the 22nd she was 745 miles behind but the next day we widened the gap again to 780 miles, despite lacking the winds we really needed. Our day's run was only 325 miles, whereas way to our north the Whitbread fleet was romping along in strong favourable winds and *Interim Justicia*, a 64-foot sloop now skippered by Lawrie Smith with Paul Standbridge in the crew, had just claimed a day's run of 428.7 miles. This was a new and very impressive world record for a monohull and to think that less than twenty years ago 300 miles was considered very fast indeed!

Gradually we began to feel the effects from the predicted bubble of high pressure. The wind lightened and backed round to the south. It even went easterly for a short period on the 24th and fell to a force 2. Meteorological garbage was the term Bob Rice used to describe the situation, adding, "With serious reservations, I'd think it worthwhile to consider heading north." We were in a jam and needed to be anywhere but here. As the wind dropped we were unable to progress fast enough to catch a depression ahead where there were strong westerlies, and 400 miles astern there was another low, bringing *Lyonnaise* in its wake and again supplying good winds. The other system which was speeding the Whitbread boats along was not that far north, but it would cost three days if we crept through the high to join it. Reluctantly, therefore, we decided to plod on eastwards at the present latitude and hope the meteorological chaos would be resolved – and before *Lyonnaise* caught up. Sooner or later the weather must return to normal, but it is sometimes hard to console oneself with this thought when averaging only 6.5 knots. The next day, the 25th, our day's run was the worst of the whole voyage, a miserable eighty-eight miles of just 3.7 knots, which meant that in two days the total was the same as sixteen hours in good westerlies. This was just gut-eating and, to rub salt into the wound, *Lyonnaise* had great sailing and narrowed the gap to 530 miles. We received a message from Paris that perhaps this was always their game plan! We knew Olivier had made a powerful impression on the media, but we wondered how anyone could imagine he had the ability to predict these conditions seven weeks in advance.

We were now just about as isolated as is possible on the planet and the Satcom picked this very moment to give up. It refused to send messages and received on an arbitrary basis. The manuals came out, the batteries were charged, we fiddled with the programme and all to no avail. Then Peter gave its brains a thump with a fist and this persuaded it to start functioning again, a lesson for the technocrats! If we had not got it working we would have lost the most convenient method of communicating because, although we had the radio to fall back on, it took longer to establish contact and lacked a fax capability. We were more than a thousand miles from any other humans except for the crew of *Lyonnaise* and the Whitbread boats and we were not moving towards habitation very fast. We were also in the unenviable position of being far further south than is normal for yachts.

In this frustrating state it was best not to think about the time slipping past and concentrate on distractions. The icebergs were around, sometimes a good number, and the sight of them always drew an audience. Ed managed to steer between two growlers which appeared to be only about sixty feet apart, at least he thought they were two separate pieces, it was hard to tell. This was not casualness on his part, sometimes the growlers showed only a couple of hundred feet ahead and by the time the message went back seventy feet from the lookout to the helmsman, it was almost too late to take avoiding action. A sixty-foot whale accompanied us for a while, then two of his friends turned up, which brightened the day, although they could also be viewed as another potential mobile obstruction. It snowed during the night, a light sprinkling over the decks – much nicer than hail. There was one major compensation however, as in muffling up to protect himself from the cold, Ed lost his voice, but the cold and condensation on the inside of the boat almost made one want the voice back if it meant we could be warm and dry again!

Of all the known fish and mammals in the oceans, none is more dangerous that the killer whale. Those likeable heroes of many an aquatic park are one of the most efficient killers on earth and must be treated with great respect. Their prey is usually seals but can be anything, whales and even the most powerful of all land carnivores, the polar bear, if they can catch one swimming. They will knock over icefloes to throw penguins into the water when hungry, and they might easily think we were a new form of seal or penguin on a form of fast-moving berg. Until now I have found they have usually swum past with hardly a glance, so the sight of a pod of eight of the creatures pursuing us on the 26th was greeted with some consternation. The wind had improved and we were making 17 knots when they appeared, having little difficulty in keeping up and making a great show of surfing on the wave tops as they followed. They looked like fast power launches at speed, throwing up large bow waves on either side. Fortunately, they must have fed recently as they did not stay for long but disappeared to look for something else to worry. What they might have made of our inflatable penguin is anyone's guess, but I'm not sure I would want to tempt them.

The winds of the 25th and 26th increased to a force 6–7 from the north-west on the 27th and we leaped forward like a frustrated coiled spring. Cold spray was again a menace, but the reward was 247 miles covered in twelve hours, which eased to a 390-mile day's run and then 475 the next day, one of the best of the whole voyage. These two days enabled us to open up to 720 miles from *Lyonnaise* and so return them to a safer distance behind. But they were 300 miles north of our latitude, and we envied them this as it was bitterly cold on deck and no one hung around to chat at the end of a spell on the wheel. Life became basic, eat, sleep and work, and there was little social inter-action. A small rise in the sea-water temperature from 2°–4°C raised hopes of warmer conditions and that we might be escaping from the iceberg area, but the sight of two bergs at 116°W, where the frequency was supposed to decrease, put paid to any such ideas, and the freezing lookout continued. One unexpected result of the long period of cold weather was that we were using more Calor gas than anticipated. A cylinder was lasting only four days here, as opposed to eleven in the tropics, and we reluctantly decided to ease up on usage. Scones and pastry disappeared from the menu, tea was rationed to one boiled kettle every three hours, but at least everyone was assured of one cup of something warm during a watch.

The good fortune which brought two such excellent days was not destined to continue. On the 28th we were warned to expect the ridge of high pressure to move south and consequently we were advised to edge south as well but be prepared for a wasteful tack north when our southerly track ran out of westerlies. This situation was forecast for within twenty-four to twenty-six hours, but first there was a front due from the north, and already on the 28th February its approach was signalled by a veering wind. At dawn we had, unusually, a clear sky except for a circle of cloud around the horizon. As we caught up with this cloud the wind fluctuated in strength and direction, but the general trend continued to be a veer, north by east at 0800, north-north-east at noon and then north-easterly later in the day as we passed another milestone, 100°W. During that evening the wind gradually increased, force 5 at midnight, force 6 at daybreak and up to a 7 by breakfast time. The barometer, which dropped 6.5 millibars between 0700 and 1200, then nose-dived from 989.5 millibars down to 981.5 by 1600. Such a rapid fall, indicating closely set isobars, creates a very steep pressure gradient and therefore strong winds. By 1300 we had a gale and were being pushed remorselessly south-east by a growing north-north-easterly sea. These short seas, and this is a relative description considering the wave size of between forty and sixty feet, were the worst we had encountered so far. The boat was shuddering horribly in the seaway whenever we hit a wave and the time was right to adopt a cruising attitude. So all hands were called and everyone piled on deck. The main was already fully reefed, so we took it down completely with three of the crew on the main boom platform to haul the sail down and lash it in a scene reminiscent of furling on a square-rigger yard, all with the accompaniment of a howling wind and spray. The storm jib had already replaced the staysail, a wet task made doubly disagreeable since the water was so cold. The speed fell to around 2 knots and we reduced the watches to two on deck. The helm was left hard over and we jogged along waiting for an improvement in the situation. Now she was not being pushed, *Enza* felt in no danger and was lying comfortably almost beam on to the seas. The odd wave hit the hull, pushing the boat bodily sideways, but these were heavy soft blows not hard slaps and were unlikely to cause any structural problems, although we were thankful for Barry's reinforcing work when one erupted beneath the godpod. We might no longer be racing but, assuming nothing broke, we were living to fight another day!

This was fascinating boat handling in circumstances not readily found anywhere else in the world. The most interesting part of it was watching how such a large boat went over the top of the waves so easily, compared with the way a smaller boat would have been tossed about. *Enza*'s size gave the impression of safety and I never believed we were seriously threatened. Although we had warps ready to stream in case the seas deteriorated and we were forced to bear off down the waves, these proved unnecessary. The front passed at about 1600 hours when the wind backed sharply from north-east to north-north-west and before nightfall we could start hoisting a little more sail and get moving eastwards again, making 11 knots.

Our day's run was unsurprisingly poor, only 136 miles, but part of this was due to yet another failure of the rolling forestay. The little grub screws which hold the aluminium extrusions together came loose again, allowing the inner and outer pieces to move until the gaps between adjacent sections in each coincided. When this happened the turn applied by the rope on a drum at the base was not transmitted along the whole forestay, with the result that the sail tore again. We ended up with two hands aloft working together to refix the extrusions, a job which took four hours, during which we were pushed south-eastwards instead of being able to lay the desired course, which was now north-east. It was not a workshop repair but then who could achieve that halfway up a forestay on a rolling boat in the Southern Ocean? The problem was probably due to the way the system was assembled and would take years to show in a boat that simply raced locally, but in the forty-four days since departure we had completed the equivalent of twenty-eight Fastnet Races non-stop, so our equipment was undergoing a particularly searching test.

Slowly we were making progress towards the next major milestone in the voyage, the rounding of Cape Horn, but the weather continued to bedevil us. The wind, having gone north-westerly for half a day late on the 1st and early on the 2nd March, returned to the north-east and we were driven back to a fine reach with a fall off in speed to an average of no more than 10 knots. Behind us even the Whitbread boats, who were also driven south, could go this fast. *Lyonnaise* was now amongst the Whitbread fleet and put out a message announcing they too had run into very bad weather and thought they were in danger of breaking up, their speed was just 2 knots, which was not unreasonable if they were hove-to. On past evidence, if they were crying wolf we could expect a sudden burst of speed to follow, so we put little faith in the story. We were right. On the 3rd when they sent this message they were 701 miles behind. A day later, although we sailed only 190 miles, they narrowed our lead to 528, 415 on the 5th, 350 on the 6th. Our comfortable advantage, which amounted to four solid days at one point, was reduced to a day or, put another way, they had taken a thousand miles out of us in 4,500 miles, and we still lacked the decent weather to put matters right. To some watching ashore it probably looked as if we had suddenly lost the ability to sail the boat properly.

We had already learned that *Enza* was a good seaboat in seas of up to fifty feet, but of course in the Southern Ocean they can be larger. How the boat would cope with anything of sixty to seventy feet was unknown and, frankly, we would rather not find out. Waves of such size would toss a lightweight platform like *Enza* effortlessly around if we hove to and the only possible way to survive was to run down wave, towing everything we had aboard behind us as a sea anchor. If the winds were from the east this would mean turning back the way we had come, straight towards *Lyonnaise*. One of the mariner's worst fears is to be at Cape Horn with a contrary wind. Usually the wind is from the west, five days out of seven on average, which favours the vessel arriving from the west. Those who attempt to get round from the Atlantic to the Pacific usually have a rough passage as, even if they are lucky and enjoy easterly winds, they rarely get clear before the westerlies catch them and ensure a very hard beat. Some of course never do get round, Captain Bligh is one of the more famous historical examples and perhaps if he had weathered the Horn, the mutiny on HMS *Bounty* might never have happened.

The 3rd March brought winds from the north-east, force 6,

accompanied by hail squalls. It was a miserable night, a falling barometer again with the apprehension of an even more easterly slant to the wind before we actually rounded the Horn. When the moon was hidden behind a cloud it was pitch dark. It was my habit before coming on watch to go to the galley and make a cup of tea, and this time I stumbled across the lurching deck in the dark whilst seeking the entrance to the port hull and at the last moment I was thrown outwards against the guard rails, which bounced me back inboard. I sat down for a moment. This was crazy. I should have connected up my safety line to the life-lines we rigged across the hull for just this purpose. It only took one slip for someone to fall overside. On a night like this, when the noise of the wind gusting to 47 knots drowned out all but words shouted close by, no one would hear a cry. They might see a flare but by the time numbed and shocked fingers found the projector, loaded and fired it, the boat would be a mile away. How long would a body stay alive in a temperature of 2°C? No, the risk was not worth taking, I had been given a reminder of the wave's power and would clip on in future.

Down in the galley I groped for the switch for the red light and put on the kettle. The noise of the sea outside was considerable and the kettle kept bouncing on the top of the stove, which was shaking with the boat, but even so tucked away in this tiny space the flimsy hull gave a wonderful false sense of security, a feeling of exclusion from the howling elements outside. I brewed up in one of the insulated mugs we bought in the USA when originally collecting the boat, which amazingly were still intact, put in sugar to allow the tea bag to draw better, an old Merchant Navy trick since I like a strong infusion, and then I clambered back on deck, eyes still unadjusted, and went carefully across to join the other two on watch in the cockpit. The tea tasted great.

Over the next few days Bob Rice had advised us to expect some easterlies but nothing too serious. We needed easterlies like a hole in the head and we blamed our predicament on him, which was very unfair. It is not easy sitting in an office studying a plethora of information coming in at all hours and then predicting exactly what might happen in a small area on the globe's surface thousands of miles away. To assist him we sent weather reports every six hours to give a feel for the local situation. The main worry was that we were already into stronger north-easterly winds than projected and the last thing we wanted was more of the same.

Initially we were slightly encouraged when, after a steady 35-knot north-easterly through the day of the 3rd, the barometer started a very gradual rise during the night, from 986 millibars in the evening to 990.2 the following morning. Hopes were raised even further when the wind backed to the north and eased to a force 5, but then the barometer began to fall again, and Bob came through with news that there was another front heading our way. The only good part of this was that the front would probably back the wind further, but first it would increase its strength. This was the worst possible situation with winds of an easterly slant and at least gale force, possibly up to storm pitch off the Horn, the old east-bound sailor's nightmare, the Southern Ocean's final throw. You can never beat this ocean. How can you hope to win against something so vast and powerful which does not even notice your presence? All you can do is survive and think yourself lucky you got away with it this time, and we had yet to achieve this.

The seas gave us the first headaches. The course was easterly whilst the wind was north but there was a residual north-easterly swell which prompted a reduction in sail to ease the pounding at daybreak. Throughout the morning we watched the wind rise very slightly and we could tell by the way the wave crests were breaking forwards that they were still building. A point might well come when they were so large we would need to slow the boat right down, so during the morning a working party of Ed, Angus and I got out the anchor chain, the longest spare ropes, such as reserve halyards, and the anchor warps. The anchor warp was doubled back on itself a couple of times and then the heavy half-inch chain attached to it. The halyards were tied to each end of this heavy mass of rope and chain. The objective was to stream the whole as a bight with 250 feet of halyard from each hull with the chain and anchor warp as the weight at the head of the bight. Ed finished off the job by sewing the ropes together to make them less liable to slipping undone. We were as ready as possible and, frankly, nobody could think of anything safer to prepare. When the waves really built up, and we had to anticipate they would, our main concern would be keeping the boat from capsizing and running too fast before the waves. The warps streamed out astern would at least stop us rushing ahead and we hoped they would provide some inertia to any capsizing force.

At noon we were just over 200 miles from the longitude of Cape Horn and the wind was a west-north-westerly at 22 knots. There was a veer to the north an hour later, accompanied by gusts of 47 knots. The only sail left set was a fully reefed mainsail but that was giving too much driving force so it was handed. Now we were being propelled solely by the wind on the mast, rigging and main boom. The waves were awkward. The residual north-easterly seas continued but were increasingly dwarfed by the fresh north-north-westers. The basic course was east-south-east, but we had to come off more and more in order to prevent the waves crashing too heavily into the port hull. The tactic was to hold her broadside on until a particularly large wave threatened, then we paid off. All this meant we were inexorably heading towards Graham Land in Antarctica and we began to consider what dubious shelter might exist behind the islands fringing the western coast of Antarctica if the wind failed to ease within the next day. Interestingly the climatic tables of the two observation posts closest to our path showed the pressure was not very different to the average expected in March and temperatures were not far out either, 1°C was the mean daily maximum on average, the minimum was 3°C lower!

Mid-afternoon saw the wind gusting at 54 knots, the top end of force 10 and a full storm, at which point the instruments decided to abdicate. In a way it was a relief, as at least we no longer frightened ourselves with the true wind speed, although I am not sure which is worse, knowing the truth or suppressing a vivid imagination! Throughout, the boat was holding up well. The larger waves were now at least sixty feet high and breaking hard against the hull, sending heavy spray across the deck and pushing the whole boat bodily sideways. Luckily they did not seem vicious, just enormous, and the sheer mass made them dangerous. We pulled up the dagger boards as they were no longer effective against the sideways thrust every time a wave struck, indeed they were applying unnecessary strain to the structure and in danger of snapping off altogether. In these circumstances it seemed better to slide sideways rather than try and hold up against the seas.

No one felt like resting and we sat around the cockpit, anchored by the safety harnesses, and watched in awe as the endless succession of waves stretched away to the horizon. These were proper greybeards, each one breaking at the crest and only differentiated by the quantity of breaking. More than once we were ready to stream the warps but each time we held back, not because it was hazardous and involved going out on to the exposed sterns to clear the warps over the steering rods connecting the two tillers, but because the boat was jogging along quietly, not speeding too much as we went down the front of the waves and recovering quickly after each particularly large surge. She felt happy, always a good sign, and we were not willing to risk an untried process until there was no other solution, although we were convinced it would work.

The alternative to streaming warps was to set the storm jib and harden up until the wind was about seventy degrees on the bow so the bows were climbing the waves. I think she would have lain all right with those waves but, of course, if a large one had knocked her sideways she would be placed across the oncoming crest, the wind would fill the sail and accelerate her, and to remedy this would have meant luffing back into the waves quickly, a nasty and dangerous manoeuvre. Another hazard of lying head to the waves is that the boat might be pushed physically backwards, putting huge strains on the rudders. So, on balance, this alternative was too risky, also the sheer size of the breaking waves would have tended to lift and capsize the boat or push her sideways into the trough in front where she would be vulnerable to the wave as it broke across the deck. Some people have suggested that a large parachute-type drogue is the answer in these circumstances. We did not possess one but it would have had to be exceptionally robust and needed extremely strong securing points aboard the boat to have withstood the tremendous snatching loads each time a wave struck.

Slowly the afternoon passed with all eyes anxiously looking for signs of an ease. The barometer stayed frustratingly steady at 986 millibars, although, as we had been unable to calibrate this since before departure from Brest, we had no way of knowing whether this was the true atmospheric pressure, but at least it showed the general rises and falls. The pressure appeared to be dragging along the bottom after a major fall and the lack of movement was not encouraging. We were waiting for a rise as after a few hours this would normally bring some relief. In fact, unbeknownst to us, the isobars on either side must have been moving apart slightly as change was on its way.

The problem with the wind instruments was discovered and rectified by 1800 hours when the wind definitely showed signs of abating. An hour later it was just west of north at 33 knots, force 7 or a half gale, and we knew by the way the wave crests had ceased breaking forward and were falling back that the wind was no longer generating the larger waves and the seas should start to subside before too long. After a gale a good rule of thumb is to allow eight hours for the waves to decline to a sensible sailing level in an average-sized cruising yacht, but we were 92 feet long and different rules prevailed. Shortly after 1830 we set the storm jib. This held the average speed at 8 knots, which we made all afternoon in the storm, but now we required more power to make the boat feel positive. She had begun to slop around due to insufficient driving force. As the easterly waves disappeared and the north-westerlies diminished, more sail became desirable and the staysail replaced the storm jib shortly before midnight and a fully reefed mainsail two hours later. As a result the pounding increased minimally but we were keen to get on. The lesson of the good drivers from the square-rig days was to push the boat hard and get round the Horn with all speed. Those who nursed their boats delayed and exposed them to the storms for longer and often ended up with more damage than the pushers. Our day's run was 221 miles, or 9 knots, whilst *Lyonnaise* managed almost double and closed to within 350 miles. We half expected this as de Kersuason had reported his boat was breaking up yet again two days previously, so we suspected all was well.

It had always been the hope to sight Cape Horn as we went past. I had not seen it for twenty-five years and was anxious to get decent photographs from the sea. Those who had been here more recently were ever keen for another view. If the Southern Ocean represents the Himalayas then Cape Horn is the Everest of the sea, the one Cape whose rounding secures respect from sailors the world over. It's not that it is constantly rough and the wind always storm force. There can be calms which leave a craft tossing about in seas big enough to have shaken the masts out of more than one square-rigger. But when it really is blowing a gale the seas are worse, due to the shallowing of the water between South America and Antarctica where it is compressed into a small area. There is no other shipping route which has such an obstacle. Very few people alive, about twenty-five in all, have sailed non-stop from Europe around Africa, past Australia to the Cape, and we were about to add eight to that number, in record time as well, but we had to calculate when we actually passed the Cape on the GPS as we were a hundred miles out to sea. The time from Ushant to Cape Horn was 48 days, 2 hours and 32 minutes, more than five days faster than *Commodore*, but the unfavourable weather we had suffered since New Zealand meant it had taken us twelve days to reach this point from the International Date Line, at an average speed of 14.75 knots instead of ten days at 17 knots as we originally planned. But all things considered, we did well to keep the average this high. We were forty-seven days out and we had thirty days in which to sail back to Ushant. *Commodore* covered this same distance in twenty-six days, we could hope for better.

Steve Anscell came out to Chile for a rendezvous, hoping to film *Enza* as she rounded the most famous cape in the world. We also had film to transmit and after the storm there was a great deal of interest from the media, so Steve located an aircraft and stood by. To fly the 120 miles out to sea from Cape Horn he made contact with a pilot used to ferrying people to Antartica, which seemed a sensible way to proceed. The aircraft was a De Haviland Twin Otter, a robust and reliable plane designed to be a workhorse in the open areas of Canada and so ideally suited for rugged work. We made contact by radio whilst it was on the runway at Puerto Williams and they quickly took off on what was to become the most alarming ten hours Steve ever spent. But by now we had come to the conclusion that he quite liked living dangerously! Which was just as well.

The normal range of an Otter is not sufficient for the Antarctic flight so the pilot had made some pretty basic modifications to turn the aircraft into a longer-range version than the manufacturers had envisaged. Strapped in place of four seats were five forty-five-gallon oil drums with pipes leading from them to the main fuel tanks! If this seems slightly hair-raising, the pilot also turned out to be a smoker. He needed a cigarette, he pointed out, to calm his nerves when flying so near enemy airspace. Whilst circling to collect our film via the micro-wave circuit, the aircraft strayed into Argentine air space, which was a serious hazard while Chile and Argentina are not on good terms. Indeed both maintain large military garrisons in Tierro del Fuego against the threat of invasion by the other. The pilot pointed out the risks, and lit up another cigarette.

We crossed the longitude of Cape Horn at 1132 ship's time on the 5th and officially entered the Atlantic part of the Southern Ocean. Now, when the wind co-operated, we would head north and into the lee of South America which would allow the first respite in thirty days from the continual Southern Ocean swell. Unbelievably, the high pressure system, which had accompanied us as a ridge, a bubble and then a ridge again all the way from New Zealand, seemed unwilling to be parted from us and was also moving round the Horn into the Atlantic, thus continuing to present a barrier that we must cross if it refused to dissipate. This was confirmed by Steve who mentioned that he saw nothing but calm seas for thirty miles south of the Horn, despite the strong squalls close to the land itself.

We were entering the last lap at a meteorological disadvantage and *Lyonnaise* was not far behind, showing an unquenchable determina-tion to make a fight of it all the way to the finish.

9

A Lazy High

With 'only' 7,500 miles to go, we laid out the chart of the Atlantic and considered the best tactics for a really fast finish. The three meteorological obstacles to the northward passage of a sailing vessel through the Atlantic are the same for a craft going the other way. The accepted method of dealing with them is identical: go right in the southern hemisphere, west rather than east at the equator, and left in the northern hemisphere. The final route to be selected was a question of degree and depended upon the precise location of the weather systems, so before launching ourselves at the first of these puzzles we had to know the whereabouts of the South Atlantic high's centre and where it was heading. The original plan was to trace the square-rig route by taking a wide sweep eastwards and round the South Atlantic high pressure, but we turned as usual to Bob Rice for confirmation.

Bob sent us a long fax which was a text book for handling a sailing boat travelling north through the South Atlantic, plus some logical conclusions based upon the current meteorological situation. No human forecaster, he said, had ever been able to show skill for projections beyond forty-eight, or maybe seventy-two hours. So in these ranges, as we were now, it was mandatory to rely on computer models for guidance. At times they do a remarkable job, at other times not, but Bob felt that on a broad scale, the US model was in the ball park maybe sixty-five to seventy per cent of the time beyond five days. The obvious flip side was that for twenty-five to thirty per cent of the time you can get caught out, particularly in circumstances like ours where, once committed, it is difficult or impossible to change tactics.

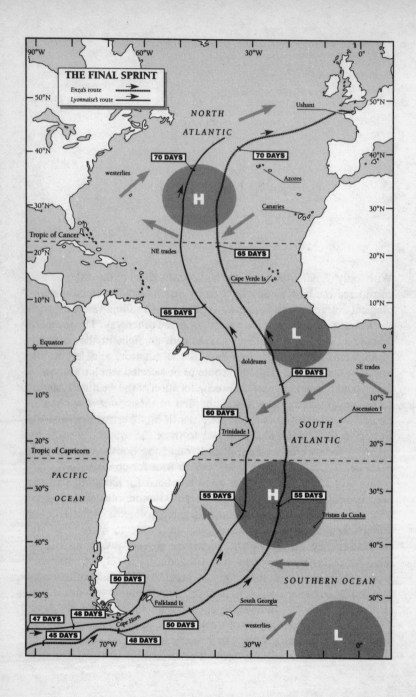

Certainly north of 45°S our options were extremely limited.

The shortest distance from Cape Horn to the equator along the line drawn from Staten Island to Recife had too many potential pitfalls, particularly for a multihull like *Enza* whose performance beating to windward was not brilliant. Tactically we must utilise the multihull's advantages and this meant finding reaching conditions. It seemed ages since we last enjoyed this situation, when *Enza* really showed her paces, and we had almost forgotten the radical difference in speeds between a reach and a beat. Primary amongst the pitfalls on the direct route was the high probability of light air or headwinds between the parallels of latitude 50° and 20°S. This would be particularly so if an existing high, blocked in place by other factors, failed to move or a new one moved across the South Atlantic, which was looking likely from the way the ridge of high which had accompanied us from New Zealand was now round the Horn. Even if we took this route there could be a considerable additional cost due to the prevailing north and north-westerly winds on the south side of the mean high ridge and north and north-easterly winds on the north side, with headwinds closer to the shore. In other words, Bob's guess was that if we headed up the coast we would run into day after day of beating conditions, so his proposal was that for the present we should aim to stay close to the traditional square-rig route, since we could dive either way from there if there was a dramatic change in the pressure systems.

Bob went on to explain that the mean high pressure ridge was typically on an axis from 30°–50° westerly longitude to south of Cape Town and the moving highs tend to follow that track eastwards. So, climatological risk areas for light air on an eastern route, the one we planned, are between 25° and 35°S. The compensation was that some of the world's most reliable trade winds are the south-easterlies on the eastern side of the South Atlantic high, but we would have to pass through the risk area to reach them. It was the difficulty of forecasting the future movements of the high beyond five days which supplied the unpredictable element and could make a total nonsense of the most carefully calculated plan. If the high stayed where it was we could safely swing round to its east and straight into the trades. If it moved after we committed ourselves to the eastern route, we could run into light winds, whereas the alternative western route, closer to the coast of South America, would then have moderate to fresh winds, albeit more headwinds than anything, but at least winds. This was the gamble we had to take and the decision could not be put off for long.

Bob reminded us that his preliminary forecast became vulnerable around 35°S on the eastern lobe of the blocked elderly high, but for planning purposes on the eastern route he proposed that we use as our waypoints 50°S/47°W, 40°S/30°W and 30°S/15°W, the last a distance from our current position of about 2,600 miles, which might take perhaps seven days. The current forecast suggested this would work, as the old high would remain planted for that period, but if it shifted we might have to go to the Greenwich meridian at 0°E/W. The overall distance on the eastern route to the equator was 5,400 miles, whereas the western alternative was about 4,600 miles. The difference, if both routes were sailed equally quickly, was two days, but the odds of losing over two days if we selected the coastal route were pretty high. However since no one could predict with any real accuracy what was likely to happen in a week's time, we should not head slavishly for the waypoint. In Bob's view there was every chance of the winds backing, so we should go for speed and avoid hardening up to force ourselves north. It would be nice to pick up distance on *Lyonnaise* but it was far more vital to get round the high before its inevitable shift eastwards.

It was as clear a synopsis of the situation as we could have hoped to receive. The background was laid out, the choices fully explained and finally there was a conclusion, but with an option left open should conditions change. We set course for the first waypoint.

Aboard *Lyonnaise* just over 300 miles behind they would be going through the same calculations but complicated by the need to discover a way of overtaking a boat with a very similar performance. If the gap were greater, there would have been no question of her having anything to lose by taking the inshore route, assuming the meteorological conditions were the same, since there was no point in joining a procession. On the other hand she had dramatically closed the gap on us recently and, in spite of the risks of the western route, they might pull off a fast one, but the odds were against it. It was perhaps better to track us and hope for superior sailing or boat speed, or slight differences in the weather along the way, such as had allowed her to catch us in the Southern Ocean. Either way she posed a worry, because the situation could change to her advantage any time but, on balance, because of the greater reliability of the eastern alternative, she was a greater nuisance if she followed in our tracks. We would have to wait until de Kersuason decided to communicate after he rounded the Horn to discover which route he would select.

Before we could grapple with the main South Atlantic high we had yet to pass the small one to our north. For the 6th, 7th and most of the 8th March the wind remained stubbornly northerly, even north-easterly at one stage. This kept us south to the extent that we did not cross the 50th parallel until the 8th, by which time we had progressed thirty degrees of longitude to 38°W with day's runs of just over 300 miles. Bob Rice eventually identified this as yet another developing bubble of high pressure close to our north, moving east at 25 knots, about twice our speed. Until it passed we could expect little change and if we attempted to go north through it, we would be stopped, so there was no alternative but to proceed with the slightly north of east course for the moment, which was not all bad as it was roughly close to the square-rig route. This bubble was already east of *Lyonnaise*, so they were free to make a good course northwards if they wished and in favourable winds. The gap between us again closed, 318 miles on the 7th, and then we were 336 miles apart on the 8th, but this was because she was steering a more northerly course and our paths were beginning to diverge. If we measured the distance that day from each boat to the equator and on to the finish, the measurement would be very close now. But this, of course, ignored the effect of winds and currents. Whilst our options were still restricted, further ahead the main South Atlantic high started to change and appeared to be developing into an east–west-running ridge. If this was the case, all our efforts to make easting might be totally wasted as there was no longer any question of going east of this high. That would mean going right over to Cape Town. We were therefore faced with slogging through it and its associated calms.

Lyonnaise would have the same problem but she was almost level now and the gamble involved in taking the western route had diminished, for the first part of the route anyway. We definitely had the good fortune and better routing when passing through the

South Atlantic high on the way out but by now *Lyonnaise* had two slabs of good luck under her belt, the first in the Southern Ocean across the South Pacific and the present one. The meteorological dice were not falling well for us and we were losing time, but if *Lyonnaise* was going well she was not ahead yet. Indeed, back at home Ladbrokes the bookmakers closed the book on the 10th March and gave our odds of breaking the record at 4:1 on.

We had not seen any icebergs for a week so thick mist, falling sea-water and air temperatures on the 7th had us back on lookout and watching the radar again. This invigorated Ed, who indulged in an orgy of spring-cleaning. We could never be sure when Ed would unilaterally decide that something was not required and chuck it overside, so we kept an eye on his activities which were, as usual, accompanied by lots of noise. Still, it made him feel better and the job, although not essential, left us tidier than before. On the domestic front the 'official' jar of lime pickle ran out. Much criticised at the beginning of the voyage on account of its weight and my peculiar tastes, just about everyone had been digging in for some time and Barry was even caught adding it to peanut butter on a biscuit! Fortunately, I had anticipated this crisis and stowed away another pot but did not reveal the fact for a day or two, just to allow everyone a chance to miss it a little and from then I released only small amounts at a time. Other items too were having to be rationed. Lavatory paper was in short supply, not because we were using more than the half roll per day we had anticipated due, perhaps, to over-indulgence in lime pickle, but because so much was ruined through damp in the Southern Ocean. But whilst some items were running low, others were relatively plentiful and one was diesel oil for the generators. These motors had consumed far less than expected, despite heavy usage, and of course the heater had failed quite early on, so we were well stocked with fuel. Oil is not something we could cast overside, even in sealed containers, so we unshipped the wind generators which reduced our windage and relied solely on the motors from now on. With diesel oil weighing about ten pounds a gallon, this also cut down weight and every little gain in this way was a small increase in speed potential. Our calculations at this stage showed that the three and a half weeks of food remaining and three and a bit bottles of Calor gas out of the twelve we started with, together with the diesel, amounted to about three-quarters of a ton of stores. This represented about 7.5 per cent of our all up weight at the start.

On the hygiene front there was still spray around from a residual north-easterly sea left by the high so I took advantage of this to have a shampoo. Clothed in oilskins with a tight rubber neck seal, I awaited the arrival of a wave over my head, applied salt-water shampoo, rubbed it vigorously and then used the following wave for a rinse. If one was really lucky a rain squall would conveniently arrive shortly afterwards, in which case one's hair seemed as soft and squeaky clean as a TV commercial. I reflected it was a pity the cleanliness stopped at the neck, but it was far too cold to strip off for a complete wash. We all waited until the 11th when the sea-water temperature was 21°C and there was an orgy of bathing, with the boat smelling a lot fresher as a result.

Meanwhile, late on the 8th, after many false starts, the wind at last came round to the north-west and we started moving properly again. This little piece of good fortune led to another as we crossed the Antarctic convergence line on the morning of the 9th and promptly ran into warmer sea-water temperatures, up from 5°–10°C in minutes – and sunlight! To cap it all we had our best day's run for a week, 456 miles on a north-east by easterly course. In fact we did not gain that much northing, but were heading quickly towards a small developing gap in the ridge of high pressure which might enable us to squeeze through.

Lyonnaise was almost on the same latitude now, only twenty miles south, in fact, but she was now definitely committed to the westerly course and was eleven degrees to the west. It remained to be seen who was right but, with a hundred per cent hindsight, if she had followed in our wake, she would probably have done better as the winds were slightly more favourable astern of us. This might turn out to be the race-deciding tactic, but with some hesitancy, due to anxiety as to the future movement of the high, we were pretty sure we were in the right place. In France the *Lyonnaise* supporters were jubilant at their boat's progress, and de Kersuason produced one of his famous quips, "Now I am going to eat apples!" This was offering hostages to fortune since the weather was so fickle, but also understandable as they had to hide their disappointment when we took a huge lead early on and, even though they gradually clawed much of it back, it had taken an awfully long time. Determining which of two competing boats is really ahead is never easy in such conditions. You may as well draw straight lines across mountains as believe a straight line is the quickest way through a complicated weather system. The whorls of isobars, denoting the high and low pressure areas, make the same barrier to a sailing boat's progress as a mountain range does to a pedestrian, although both look flat on a map. We were on the traditional, safer route, *Lyonnaise* was taking a risky gamble and whereas our way must offer winds sooner or later, there was no such guarantee for them.

Our confidence proved well founded on this occasion, as we did another good day's run on the 10th with 469 miles. *Lyonnaise* covered only 273 miles in the same period, perhaps a warning against shouting before the finish line was reached! Not that anyone had cause to shout at this juncture as both boats still had to pass the high and anything could happen. Our run brought us across the 40th parallel, which officially placed us into the South Atlantic and out of the Southern Ocean. It was thirty-eight days since we had crossed the same line going south.

We struck an object with the port dagger board during the early hours that morning. Shades of previous accidents and why did they always happen in the South Atlantic? The board was withdrawn, rather like a rotten tooth, but fortunately there was no damage and no leaks developed through the casing. Whatever had hit passed behind and away and since it was dark we had no way of telling whether it was fishy or discarded rubbish drifting around. It may well have been driftwood which the port hull had ridden over until it reached the board, but something softer was more probable in view of the lack of harm. Angus sighted a whale spout astern much later in the day and the day before we had seen a seal sleeping on the surface, which seemed somewhat out of its territory. Either creature would have been injured by the collision – the seal possibly killed, but I'm not sure what one can do about warning them, except perhaps leave the echo sounder switched on, as it uses a sound wave which might attract their attention.

In the early hours of the 11th we crossed our outward route, which is known as tying the knot. It is a fairly meaningless method of measuring progress or speed as it is so dependent upon the course taken to suit the wind conditions but, for the record, we did it in 39 days, 5 hours and 51 minutes through the position 36° 46.15'S and 25° 55.9'W. At this stage we were approaching the ridge of high pressure and this was where Bob said we should push northward and drift through to winds the other side. True to prediction, the wind suddenly died. We could not hope for *Lyonnaise* to be similarly affected, she could well press on for a day or two yet, so here was an opportunity for her to gain the lead, but we hoped only temporarily. We were consoled by the fact that the weather picture showed they would run into light headwinds before long off the south-east corner of Brazil – but we weren't about to tell them that!

In the meantime we made the best of a bad job and used the calms to check over the sails, in particular the mainsail, which was normally in use and only came down completely in extreme conditions when we were unable to work on it anyway. We dropped it down and examined it minutely for chafe, taped up one or two bad points and tightened screws on the track slides which held it on to the mast. Considering the work it had done, the sail was in remarkable shape and showed little signs of the 20,000-odd miles of hard usage it had received. Sail materials are constantly being improved and they have changed beyond all recognition in the last twenty-five years. I had to replace the mainsail on *Suhaili* long before this on my circumnavigation, whereas *Enza*'s Spectra sail looked, for the most part, practically new. Of course it had only done fifty-four days, whereas at this stage in my 1968–9 voyage I had been at sea for 240 days. Barry resecured the screws holding the forestay together yet again. We could easily run out of Lock-tite for the job if the system kept falling apart at this rate. Then we all washed and had a swim in the clear blue water. Looking back at the boat it looked like Widow Twankey's laundry with washing and bedding airing all over the deck!

The sudden arrival of hot weather made me realise I was the only member of the crew who did not possess a sun hat. We had all been given them in New Zealand but mine vanished during the tour. Suddenly the direct rays were becoming offensive, so I started sewing one out of Spectra material. It took a few days to complete, was never going to be a threat to a reputable firm of hatters, but served its purpose and the material ensured it was strong enough to survive a direct hit by an exocet missile!

At this stage Bob Rice's interpretation of the weather was that we were on a col between the original centre of the high and a new one which was moving to join it, which explained why the wind died so abruptly. This being the case he expected the wind to stabilise from the north-west within the next six to nine hours. He added, "That's the realistic solution but don't know if it's the right one. Hope so, because there's not much else in immediate sight." In fact when the wind picked up in the afternoon to a force 1, it was from the north-east and stayed that way all night, apart from a few hours when it went northerly and we tacked to take whichever course gave most progress to the north.

Whilst the boat was in motion it created a draught of air across the sail's surface which enabled us to create 'lift' and keep moving. But if the boat was allowed to slow down and ultimately stop, it took time to persuade the flapping sails to settle into providing driving force again. Sailing in such light airs is hard work and requires concentration. Anyone can sail a boat when there is wind – the challenge and skill come in moving in light to non-existent airs.

A pink sky after sunset, and what was becoming a ritual look-for-the-green-flash party was followed by dinner, made by Barry who produced a lethal pudding, chocolate mousse reinforced with rum. We had hardly had an alcoholic drink since leaving Hamble, indeed there were only three bottles aboard as far as I was aware, and such was our lack of recent familiarity with spirits that Jaws identified this one as whisky! Food was, as usual, a dominating theme. I decided that as my waistline showed no sign of diminishing after fifty days, I would have a spoonful less at each meal. At the same time Ed noticed his legs were getting thinner, quite usual at sea where there are no distances to walk, and so thought he needed feeding up a bit. We agreed he could have my discarded spoonful in the quest to increase his weight. The lack of leg exercise is always a problem on a long voyage. When I completed my single-handed circumnavigation my ankles tired after walking a couple of hundred yards as they had so little work for 312 days. People think that standing gazing at the horizon on the deck of a rolling boat will exercise the legs, but it doesn't.

Ever since I realised my eyes could no longer see the small-printed soundings on a chart, I have used spectacles for reading. It is a nuisance since they are not necessary for anything beyond eight feet from my face, so I keep taking them off, putting them down, and then forgetting where I have left them. The opposite can occur and I sometimes wander off wearing them. On the 12th I did just that and walked into the runner, which knocked the spectacles off. They bounced from the trampoline on to the deck and then the wind caught them and carried them off towards the side of the hull. My frantic dive was four inches short in the end and I watched them topple into the sea. Fortunately, I had spares, but only half-lenses which were not as strong. I suppose there was consolation in that if the eyes had to work harder they might improve. I normally find my sight does get better at sea anyway. The reason for crossing over to the hull with spectacles was to give myself a haircut. After nearly two months I was looking like a Sudanese refugee. I did the cut anyway, which decreased windage a little, and the loss of spectacles allowed me an excuse for not making a very good job of it!

To make a change, and allow David and Peter the opportunity to discuss America's Cup business, we altered the watch-keeping rota. Unfortunately, this meant that my watches and Ed's did not coincide, which would not normally have been a problem, except that it affected my prospects of having any peaceful sleep. I asked Ed if he would mind trying to be a little quieter, but that just encouraged him. Retaliation was swift. I persuaded Barry and Jaws to dance a short *pas de deux* over Ed's bunk when he was taking a spell below – Ed got the message and thereafter life was more peaceful.

The sticky high really was threatening the whole programme now. We had slightly over twenty-one days to finish the voyage, or achieve an average of 258 miles per day, nearly 11 knots, which was well within our capabilities, but we had travelled only 578 miles in the last three days. We needed some decent winds from the beam because once free of the high we should have good helpful winds up to the equator. There were still two obstacles left once we cleared the present one, and if the ITCZ and/or Azores high dumped on us the way the South

Atlantic one had, we would be very pushed to arrive home in time. We were coming to what was theoretically the least favourable section of the voyage from the wind point of view, plus there was always the nagging worry of damage or other unforeseen problems which might cause delays.

The dominant issue each day was the position of *Lyonnaise*, had she gained or lost against us, and Bob's latest meteorological projections for us both. News on either front was awaited with impatience. Having been proved wrong by the uncooperative high pressure system, Bob sent us a message the next day, the 13th, as follows: "Interesting sequence of winds last twenty-four hours, but it all seems to fit – finally. Trough has split the high, but in the process penetrated north-west far enough that the col actually has gone by to your north. So, good forecast, except for 180° error as your wind was 270° at 5 knots instead of 090° at 5 knots. Temporary setback! Would think that's the end of variability and that winds now continue to back all the way to south-east over the next twelve to twenty-four hours."

This sounded more like it and, in fact, it was unimportant whether the wind was east or west as we made the same amount of northing either way. Bob's candour was refreshing and I always find it rather reassuring when someone can admit to a mistake, even better when they explain why. Could we have done better ourselves? None of us on board thought so. The situation had really been a nightmare to predict. In fact, examining the movement of very shallow high pressure systems by means of satellites and computers, from a long way off as always, means putting faith in some very weak indicators.

He went on to forecast that the high, which was now south of us at last at 34°S, would become a ridge and stabilise at 30°S, roughly where we were that day. Yet another unfavourable system following us! His advice was to continue heading north and east rather than west, as the ridge was expected to turn on its axis and line up north-west/south-east to our west. East of this ridge the winds were likely to be south-easterly, west of them north-easterly. This could be the crunch, as *Lyonnaise* was west of the forecast axis and we were to its east. We would be reaching, whilst they were beating and we all knew what that meant. In fact the wind did fill in from the east and speed rose from 6 – 12 knots as a result.

In the meantime *Lyonnaise* was still going quite nicely and chose this moment to pile on the pressure. We were clearing the ridge at last and on the 14th had a run of 270 miles. But she managed 350 on the same day however, Bob was relaxed and said they were heading into a hole, an expression used to describe an area of no wind, whereas he was sure we would shortly be in the south-east trade winds. Soon after there were cheering signs to support this with an increase in the cotton balls of cumulus cloud, and the wind steadied. The exchange of positions with *Lyonnaise* at 0800 on the 15th showed we were holding steady on each other, but at 1,300 the picture was entirely different. She had suddenly slowed and headed north-east at 8 knots, whilst we were making east of north at 16 knots. This told us she had run into headwinds and the only way to proceed was to crawl towards and across the axis. Just as on the way south, we had gained at least a day, possibly more, by more accurate weather-routing.

There were no clever tactics needed now until we arrived at the inter-tropical convergence zone and we happily reached north. Squalls accompanied us during the night, occasionally rising to 19 knots, when we bore away to reduce wind pressure. Bob explained these gusts were due to nocturnal destabilisation of the air mass and we assumed he knew what he was talking about! It could be caused by anything he liked, provided it allowed us to press on at 16 knots, and the 0800 *Lyonnaise* position was eagerly awaited. When it arrived we were jubilant. They remained on the wrong side of the axis and at noon, after a 381-mile day, we were 879 miles from the equator whilst they had 1,166 miles to go. Their gamble on cutting the corner had failed, and they were in an area off the south-eastern corner of Brazil where calms are quite frequent. To make matters worse for them the axis they must cross had moved north. After all the stick we received about them drawing level, we could be forgiven for enjoying their discomfiture.

We maintained the good progress, the day's run for the 16th had been 380 miles to *Lyonnaise*'s 170, on the 17th we did 383 miles to 202 and the next day, when we crossed the equator, 364 to their 273. They omitted to give a position for the 19th, which suggested they were enjoying some wind, but we were less worried now. Morale was high, the sun was hot and I was thankful for my hat. Jaws had a sudden burst of energy and decided to finish his Yacht Master (Ocean) course. He started taking meridian altitudes of the sun, the method used to calculate latitude at noon and we knew he was serious when he delayed having lunch for the purpose. There were communal treats on the agenda as well, since we had two birthdays coming up, mine on the 17th March and David's the next day. We each had reserved goodies to celebrate, in my case a bottle of whisky and a cake baked by my daughter, while David's parcel contained a brown cake mix with candles, lollipops, a whisky cake and Maltesers. The tablecloth that came with the kit failed to prevent crumbs and spilt tea getting all over the place and in the confusion George ate Ed's slice of cake, which led to much muttering. David managed to blow out thirty-nine candles in one puff, which was not bad for an ageing youth!

Jaws, Barry and I were on watch as dusk fell with still no sighting of the green flash, but shortly afterwards a large flying fish swooped in over the bow, hit the mainsail, bounced off the main boom and landed near my bare feet in the cockpit. I had the wheel and leaped into the air to avoid the floundering fish, Jaws scuttled to the other side of the cockpit and it was fisherman's son Barry who calmly bent down, picked up the fish and flung it back into the sea. Jaws then started to pull my leg about lack of dancing ability before he became distracted with his usual concerns and enquired how flying fish were best cooked! For those who sail the tropics the answer is to boil them to remove the flesh, as they are very bony, and then make them into a fish pie or fish cakes. We could have done this at any time but somehow we never got round to it.

We knew progress would slow again at some stage in the near future, and on the 18th the wind began to back from south of east towards north-east, a sure sign that we were coming to the ITCZ. We were unsure how wide it was at this time, perhaps 300 miles, and we could not hope to pass straight through without pause, as we had managed on the way out. That would have been too lucky. But if the zone were on the move from north to south, we might minimise the delay as it would pass over quickly. If, on the other hand, the zone was moving from south to north we would accompany it, which would entail an extremely slow passage. The advance indications were that it was lying at the southern edge of its terrain between 0°–1° S, and there were two lines of convection at about 25° and 32° W. It had been static for a while, which was bad news, as its most likely next move would be northwards. Bob warned of strong squalls in thunderstorms and was proved right as usual when we had a gust of 35 knots on the evening of the 18th. Fortunately there was plenty of notice as these mini-storms came with towering cumulus clouds, usually shedding heavy rain which showed up well on the radar.

We soon learned that with a multihull it paid to go to the east of these clouds where the wind was less. If we passed on the west we received the full force of the sudden wind gusts, plus heavy rain and, much as we welcomed cool fresh water, we usually had to furl away the headsail completely to run through the squall. Being caught with too much sail set in these circumstances was the recipe for a capsize. The rain did bring a couple of benefits, apart from cooling down the boat and making the sleeping accommodation more bearable, as it washed the salt out from all the blocks and ropes, removing squeals from the former and making the latter a little more pliable.

Just after midnight on the 19th March we crossed the equator. We took 13 days, 9 hours and 3 minutes from the longitude of Cape Horn, two hours longer than *Commodore* the previous year. We had been at sea for 54 days, 7 hours and 11 minutes so far and covered 22,350 miles. This gave us nearly twenty-five days to reach the finish line, but we had only jumped one of the Atlantic meteorological hurdles, two remained to clear and we were just coming to the next one. However, analysing our tactics from the Horn, it was hard to see what might have been done differently. Perhaps if we had gone a touch further east, we would have picked up the south-east trade winds sooner, but there was no guarantee we would have passed the high any faster. The decision to take the old square-rig route had proved to be correct and we had actually opened up a little on *Lyonnaise*. But now anything could happen again. My diary for the 19th March says it all:

Our hopes that we might have a speedy sprint through the ITCZ were as speedily dashed. By the time I went on watch again at 0300 the wind was northerly about 4 knots and we were making west-north-west at 6 knots. This decreased as the night progressed. We have been warned that there is little wind on the eastern side of the convection clouds, so all night we waited expectantly for a cloud to the east to close up. Plenty of lightning from it, which encouraged the thought that wind might be there. In the meantime warm and humid. Had a sea-water wash at 0500 using a bucket and salt-water shampoo. Felt much better afterwards.

Very heavy showers at 0800 but no point in freshing off as we were completely flat becalmed an hour later and the only relief from the heat was in the ocean. Light variable winds, very frustrating.

Bob Rice says that the satellites show a band of cloud coming towards us from the north-east and he thinks that once this is past we shall be into the trades. Hope so. Lyonnaise *has averaged more than 14 knots since noon yesterday straight up the Brazilian coast, so has closed up about 150 miles. Our long-term weather prospects do not look brilliant. Firstly when we do get beyond this cloud bank to the trades they are expected to be from about 040 degrees at 20–25 knots, so hard slog to windward. Then the Azores high is wandering and a lump of it is expected to be over the southern UK in nine days, so it looks as if we may have light winds at the end. We are going to be made to work for every inch of this voyage.*

Some relief from the heat about 1430, and that wind steadied in from the north-north-east. Cool and boat speed. Celebrated by cooking everyone curry. Sun burned nose.

We could not have been more ill-fated. The ITCZ had flopped on us and started to shift north and we were doomed to drift with it in light winds instead of cracking off in the north-east trades as we had hoped, whilst behind us, yet again, *Lyonnaise* was closing the gap in better conditions. Another new race was about to begin for the final 4,000 miles home.

10

Sprinting with the Brakes On

Our lead over *Lyonnaise* was a mere 210 miles when she crossed the equator on the 20th March only a day and a half behind. Progress was desperately slow as we were beginning to feel the effects of the north-east trades, slightly more northerly at the outset; the question was how quickly would *Lyonnaise* pick up the same winds, and that depended upon the undisciplined movements of the inter-tropical convergence zone.

Before us now lay 1,500 miles of the north-east trade winds, usually steady and dependable and averaging about force 4, or 16 knots. They were called trade winds because of their reliability and were familiar to sailors from Phoenician times. The Portuguese explorers in their quest for the Cape of Good Hope had depended upon them and Columbus used their predictability to drive him, as he thought, towards China. It was these winds which gave a record run on the outward passage but now we were heading into them and could not anticipate particularly speedy sailing. To sail fast we needed to steer a course to the north-west, but this would entail making a huge loop in the North Atlantic which would carry us almost to Bermuda. Since this added a huge number of miles to the distance to go, we would need to sail almost twice as fast as a boat taking the traditional route which is close-hauled and on as near a northerly course as the wind allows. The north-east trades are not constant from that direction and the wind veers slowly round to the east as progress north is made.

The standard method of sailing through them from the south is to set a course west of north initially, which normally drives the boat to

38°–40°W, and then, as the wind veers, the course can be brought round to north and even east of north. The winds ultimately bring the boat into the influence of the Azores high pressure system and the objective is usually to pass round to its west in order to join the westerly winds which are the prevailing wind in the northern North Atlantic. The potential trouble comes from the erratic movements of the Azores high, which can extend west to Bermuda and result in a block of calms right across the Atlantic, similar to the South Atlantic high in the southern hemisphere. So with no cause to take a massive gamble, we stuck to our original intentions and proceeded along the traditional route. We waited with interest to see *Lyonnaise*'s intentions.

We were definitely in the trades on the 21st, averaging nearly 15 knots into a lumpy sea. The waves were coming in clearly defined bands from the north, north-east and north-north-east, as if caused by different currents. The general direction of the current in this area is westerly, but there are swirls. This meant the boat was wet on deck as we bashed into the waves and we adjusted speed by altering the tension on the sheets to suit whatever waves we were meeting, increasing in the calm patches, easing in the rougher ones. There were still noticeable variations in wind strength on either side of clouds, light on the west, heavier on the east, which periodically caused us to reduce sail. Moving sails around to change the trim definitely helped the motion, and we found that by putting them behind the forward weather beam we reduced the slapping considerably. The boat had now done the equivalent of thirty-seven Fastnet Races without a pause and we had to be a little cautious about the gear because we had come too far to take silly risks.

There were days of clean, clear air and on others the wind betrayed its Saharian origins by carrying a great deal of sand, which got everywhere and created a reddish-brown mud when it collected and got wet. This sand had remarkable aerodynamic properties since it must have remained in suspension for at least 1,100 miles, the distance to the nearest land upwind. The sea was very warm and contained jellyfish, the dangerous Portuguese men-of-war, a twelve-foot shark who drifted past forty feet from the hull and the inevitable flying fish. The latter scored three hits separately on Ed, Jaws and David. The latter was suitably indignant since he was on the helm and felt I should have shielded him as I was standing to weather of him at the time!

News from *Lyonnaise* on the 21st suggested her movement was somewhat erratic. We plotted her as sailing west at 8.7 knots between 0800 and 1100 and then she suddenly went at 17 knots on a course of west-north-west for the following two hours to the next position she gave. The inconsistent speed might be explained by a pause to repair damage, but the course was about as good as they would make in north-easterly winds which Bob Rice reported extended as far as 10°N, a fact we confirmed when we passed north of this latitude that day and the wind began to veer. Perhaps Olivier de Kersuason received similar reports. At all events he announced next day he was not giving his position for the next two days for "tactical" reasons. He is famous for behaving eccentrically but this decision was baffling. He needed our position much more than we needed his, as we were in the lead, and this sort of action was asking for retaliation in kind. We discussed doing just that but concluded it wasn't necessary. His choices were simple, follow us north and hope to catch up in the approaching calms of the high pressure ridge which would be a lottery for both of us, or take the wide sweep west, the extreme chance. Since he was only 300 or so miles behind, if I were he I would have continued the chase, putting on pressure which could cause breakages and knowing there was a fifty per cent chance of better wind through the ridge. However, de Kersuason had taken wild chances before and we suspected he was covering up the dramatic but risky gambit of the wide westerly loop, what might be termed the Bermudan option. If so, why keep quiet about it? The world appreciates a sporting gamble. But since it added at least a thousand miles to the distance to run, we needed to be stopped for four days for him to succeed. Only time would tell if our guess was right and, although it would always have been nice to know the whereabouts of the competition, we had plenty to occupy our minds until he came on net again.

The danger of over-pushing at this late stage was brought home that afternoon when a large stainless steel shackle parted on a starboard runner block, the sole restraint to prevent the mast toppling forward. Fortunately, we had safety strops backing up the tackles and of course the mainsail and its sheet also provide support. When items of equipment, meant to have a safe working load of some 25,000 pounds, start to break, it challenges every single part of the rig, since faith in the whole structure is shaken. Two days later Ed noticed a crack in another shackle, again on the starboard runner, and it was replaced. This shackle was nearly cracked right through. As a result all the shackles on board were checked and no cracks were found, but the breakages did not stop. The effect was, inevitably, to make us cautious.

We were now into the Azores high avoidance game. In the 1977 Whitbread I took *Condor* out on a wide westerly sweep to get around the high after we had watched its movements for two weeks and realised it was moving across to Spain about every five days. Ahead of us Eric Tabarly in *Pen Duik* went straight for the islands and was soon joined by Rob James in *Great Britain II* who had been level with us. For two days they both crept forward whilst we were almost stopped as the high dithered and then, fortunately for my credibility, it started to shift. Whilst they basked in sun and calms we picked up the westerlies and led the fleet to the finish line. The situation was different this time as the centre was in its usual place but a ridge extended all the way across the Atlantic to Antigua, and another high was due to move into the area to broaden the ridge. This would effectively create a barrier to northward motion right across the Atlantic and we could perhaps be forgiven for thinking that these transatlantic extended highs, both north and south, were more of a meteorological feature than is normally admitted. However, Bob considered that a frontal trough ahead of the new high might form a col between the two centres of high pressure roughly 30°N/40°W on about the 25th March where the wind would be non-existent. He recommended we press on northwards and plan to pass thirty degrees north-east of 37°W, where we should find easterly or south-easterly winds and could place ourselves east of the col.

None of the crew had ever been at sea non-stop this long before except myself, and that was alone where there were no opportunities for character clashes. But despite eight strong characters living in crowded living conditions, which might be considered a recipe for argument and dissension, we got on pretty well throughout the voyage. As we sailed through the trades, though, Peter commented on how quiet Ed had become, probably due to having exhausted all topics of conversation. Personally, I thought it was more like a spring being wound up and he would break out in loud pronouncements at any moment. Not that it mattered since we tolerated odd idiosyncrasies, laughed at foibles and, apart from a couple of blasts by Ed, no one had shown any irritability with anyone else.

The moment the northbound sailor awaits in the north-east trades is when the wind begins to veer east. On the 22nd we had east-north-easterlies and sailed 361 miles, on the 23rd they were round slightly to the east and we made 384 miles. We had given away a little westing during the run north from the ITCZ, about four degrees, but the overall results showed this was a good trade. The wind was at an awkward strength for us, just on the gap between the envelopes of two sails, the genoa and the jib top. When it eased we changed to the genoa for more power, when it rose we were over this sail's limits and were forced to change down. Each change took ten minutes, even with everyone up, and that assumed nothing went wrong or no new breakages occurred. The roller furling was now extemely tired and its extrusions needed resecuring even more often. On one of the changes on the 23rd we noticed that the lug which attached the system to the halyard was cracking and so this was lashed up with rope. We had thought it simply weak, but you only had to look closely to realise the lug was made from smaller diameter rod to the shackles attached to it. We wondered why. The time spent by our team putting this small error right was out of all proportion to the actual cost of the equipment. Not that we were alone in having this sort of trouble. There was a message from *Lyonnaise* explaining, why their speed suddenly jumped from 8–17 knots the last time they communicated. Their main halyard had broken. They sent someone aloft to fix it, but it broke again and they had to make further repairs. The message did not include an updated position. However, one thing we could be certain of, and it saved us from losing sleep, was that if they were true to form, they would be shouting from the rooftops the moment they were anywhere near us.

Our latitude on the 24th was 26°N and Bob Rice was urging us on by saying that for the next two days the westerlies would be at 40°N, north of the axis of the ridge which now lay from 27°N/40°W–40°N/

20°W, but then the new high would come in at about 36°N/25°W on the 27th. In other words hurry north. We were 840 miles from the 40th parallel, so we needed to average 17.5 knots to meet Bob's requirements and we had not achieved such a speed since the 10th March, two weeks before. *Commodore* had managed this rate in the same part of the ocean but the weather conditions had obviously been different the year before. We were in a race against the high towards a small featureless patch of ocean and the penalty if we lost was an indeterminate period of slow days during which the clock would continue its count-down and *Lyonnaise* might suddenly emerge in front. If we could somehow connect with these westerlies the reward would be arrival home within five days and a near fantastic seventy-day circumnavigation. At this stage, however, the odds were firmly with the high. We did a 350-mile day on the 24th with lightening easterly winds, and 262 on the 25th when the wind swung south and then veered six points almost westerly as a front passed. Our hopes rose, perhaps this was the high going slightly south and we were now into the beginning of the steady westerly winds? The arrival of the front coincided with Jaws being warned that he would have no scones that afternoon if he failed to maintain the speed at 17 knots. The speed increased immediately, due in fact to a mild squall, but we came to the conclusion that if we had fed him scones on these terms from the start, we would have arrived home a week earlier! Another bonus was that the lashings of fresh water which came with the front gave an opportunity to wash properly.

A pod of six sperm whales followed soon after, giving away their presence by blowing on the surface. The Azores used to support a small whaling industry, employing proper whalers, the long sleek rowing boats which were adapted by the British Navy as seaboats on account of their wonderful sea-keeping qualities. They had not caught many each year, but were one of the few places, like Bequia and Greenland, where whaling was permitted for a while after the ban came in. The Azoreans have not actually hunted for more than twelve years, perhaps because the numbers taken and the dangers involved made it unprofitable and there is now little demand for whalemeat, less for blubber and none at all for the balleen plates which used to stiffen ladies' corsets. Every time I pass through these waters I invariably see whales. We were surprised by our next visitor the following day though. Around mid-afternoon we felt a shudder and found something large caught around the starboard rudder by our forward motion. Investigation showed it was struggling and a closer look revealed a small shark, six to seven feet long, which was caught almost exactly midway along its length so it lay balanced and trapped. The boathook was produced and the shark prodded and pushed until it came free, and swam off, apparently undamaged.

The shark at least gave George a new subject to film, the whales blowing on the surface being a bit far away for anything epic. He had become inspired again with the approach of another film pick-up, our first since Cape Horn and the last before the finish. Whilst looking for fresh subjects he asked to be put up the mast and on his descent reported finding red sand still caught in odd places from the Saharian blow a week before.

By Saturday the 26th, the wind had eased and veered to the north, a sure sign that in fact we were on the easterly edge of the high and not past it, as we hoped. As the day progressed it continued to veer, indicating that we were also south of the centre, in which case we had lost our race with it. Both of the Atlantic calm systems had now dumped on us and we were losing valuable time, but we could not really complain. If luck is meant to average out, our good luck on the first half of the voyage was bound to be replaced by less attractive conditions now. The day's run was 265 miles, nearly 11 knots, which was good in the circumstances, but we were slowing. The forecast from the United States Coastguard confirmed the high was almost exactly on our latitude, 35°N, and 250 miles west moving towards us at 15 knots. If we squeezed a little north maybe we could recover something from the situation, but Bob Rice thought we should try to head west-north-west as it carried us across the axis of the high and into westerlies more quickly.

There were certainly strong winds around somewhere as a large residual twenty-foot swell was coming in from a very large storm to the north-west and throwing the boat around, which reduced the efficiency of the sails. Well, we wanted wind but not storm force, although if we became seriously becalmed we might be sufficiently frustrated and imprudent enough to start praying for any sort of wind!

Around the equinoctial, the 23rd March, has always been considered a dangerous time of year, when the sun crosses the equator on its march north and officially ends winter in the northern hemisphere. Traditionally this, and the 23rd September when it heads south again, are reckoned to be times of awful weather. Statistically this is a myth, but the wind is often strong enough during these parts of the year to encourage caution as far as I am concerned. In the meantime we drifted, making just over 5 knots throughout the day and night, the only consolation being that the wind, such as it was, did steady from the south-west during the morning.

We finally became frustrated and annoyed by *Lyonnaise*'s persistent failure to broadcast a position, so we clammed up too on the 27th, having not given the wind direction and force the previous day either. It seemed unreasonable that we should play by the rules and they not. The response was speedy. On the 27th they gave a position at last and we were delighted to learn they were over 600 miles to our south-west, well into the calms in the ridge behind the high. We were pleased with this, since we were only 1,600 miles to the finish now and they needed to sail a third faster to beat us to the line. Later on they released a series of positions for their silent period and we learned they had not taken the Bermudian option after all. Their course showed they had simply done a more westerly sweep than we had, a rather indecisive move which gained them nothing. Bob Rice commented rather aptly, "The French secret weapon seems to have been something less than a breakthrough. Would guess that their strategy probably buys them a pretty miserable day or two coming up." He also instructed us to get north of 42°N a.s.a.p. to avoid yet another high ridge axis, but thereafter predicted 15 knots of south-westerly winds by evening and 30 knots by midnight.

Early in the morning of the 28th we were making about 22 knots on a northerly heading towards a front which would bring north-north-westerly winds which would be less favourable. If we gybed, the new course would be straight for the finish line and would keep us with the present south-westerly winds for longer. This would also take us further from a developing depression which was giving storm force winds in the central Atlantic. Since these storms tend to move north-easterly, the further east we went the less should be the strength of the wind, although Bob was predicting that we would not avoid it completely. We put a radio call through and asked his advice, which was to gybe if we wished, but in doing so we must expect some continued effects from the high. We decided to take the risk. The winds seemed steady so all hands were called and we gybed. Despite sailing a dog's leg we made 321 miles in the twenty-four hours up to noon, but the front reached us mid-morning, accompanied by torrential rain, the wind veered quickly to the north and then north-east and we were left wondering whether we should not have gybed even earlier and got extra miles in to the east. Still, if we were grumbling, our troubles were minor compared with those of *Lyonnaise*, who sailed only 148 miles during the same period.

As we made our way to the north of the Azores, Steve Anscell was having another of his adventures. He had chartered an aircraft in Lisbon but it lacked the range to fly 800 miles direct to the Azores, so they went the 500 miles to Madeira instead. From there he flew to San Miguel in the Azores, but was still short of range as he was not allowed to refuel at the air base at Lajes. This put him under time pressure, which was not helped by difficulties in locating us and also by humidity affecting his equipment. However, he eventually managed to pick up twenty-five minutes of film, which was the best that circumstances allowed. Thankfully, this was his last hazardous long-distance flight over the sea.

Whilst this was going on, all the signals indicated we might be catching up the front again, and Bob confirmed this in a way by announcing that its axis had swung east/west and we would soon cross it. Although this brought the wind round to the south-west, which suited us, a depression was moving our way and a ship 850 miles to the west was reporting winds from the south-south-west at 46 knots. Whilst this depression with its storm force winds was due to pass north of Scotland, a trailing low would follow it into Northern Ireland. So the good news was that the wind would be from a favourable direction, the bad news was there was to be an awful lot of it.

The storm caught us on the morning of the 30th, with gusts of up to 55 knots which pushed us into surges of 27 knots. When these gusts became more frequent and the surfs more aggressive we took in all sail and continued under bare poles for a while. Speed was reduced, but only to 14 knots, a clear proof of the wind's strength and how easily the boat could be driven. The motion was quite comfortable, despite the odd wave sweeping in from astern and breaking beneath us, sending water spurting up through the trampoline and making life very wet on deck. Conditions aboard worsened as the sea became more confused, with waves coming in from every direction between south and north-west. Water was streaming into the cockpit and flooding it from ahead, both beams, as well as astern, and we were glad the escape hatch allowed it to drain away very quickly. On occasions the whole boat sat on a wave and it felt as if the godpod would break loose and float away. Progress was good though, our first day's run in excess of 400 miles for twenty days, and *Lyonnaise* was now over a thousand miles astern.

We had been at sea nearly seventy-three days and were only 617 miles from the finish line. Our time from south of Tasmania in Australia to the Lizard looked like being forty-four days, compared with the best clipper ship run for the same distance, by the *Cutty Sark*, in seventy-one days in 1887–8, almost the same time as we looked like taking for the whole circumnavigation. All the team's hard work over the previous ten weeks now gave us six days in hand to break the record, we could average 4 knots all the way to Ushant if we wished and still beat *Commodore*, although 8 knots might be more sensible, since *Lyonnaise* could catch the wind and smash *Commodore*'s time as well. This huge lead meant there was no reason to push the boat, a point which was brought home forcibly the next morning when we 'fell down the mine' again and came up all standing. Thankfully, there were no injuries on this occasion, although Jaws was ejected from his bunk and I was crumpled up like a sardine in the forward end of mine. George did not even wake up! Although the wind reduced to a force 7, the seas were increasingly anarchic, so we reduced sail for the rest of the night. Despite this we had a 380-mile day leaving just 233 miles to go.

After breakfast, as the wind and waves were increasing, we prepared the warps and chain, exactly as we had for the Horn. The forecasts were universally horrible and Bob Rice told us the depression was at hurricane force, which explained the forty- to fifty-foot waves we were having to surmount. We rigged the warps up ready to stream and did not have long to wait. Mid-afternoon, when the wind was a force 9, we fell down the mine again, this time winding David and shooting Angus straight out of his bunk into the forward end of the galley, which gave him a few bruises. We placed the heavy part of the warp, which was the anchor chain, on the port hull aft, keeping clipped on as waves were continuously pouring over the deck. The halyards which connected this to the boat were led over the steering rods so all we had to do was kick the chain out beneath the rods and allow the strain to be taken by the halyards, led through blocks on eye bolts near the stern and through the main sheet traveller outhaul blocks to the winches in the cockpit. The effect was dramatic. The halyards came taut and the boat braked immediately and lost her excessive liveliness. She felt much happier and, instead of every wave being a threat, suddenly we felt able to relax a little. Great green waves powered in from astern, breaking continuously as they came, but harnessed to our bight we crawled comfortably over them, just occasionally doing small rushes forward which tossed even our heavy chain out of the water and thereby removed the brake momentarily. It is not often one sees a hundredweight of chain flying through the air, and I suppose we could have added the anchor if matters had deteriorated, but these spurts were short-lived and the chain was not airborne for long.

It was a long wet night with the wind showing a gust of 69 knots and it was hard to relax sufficiently to sleep, since the excitement of arriving home also kept us alert. At daybreak we had company. The French were making an occasion of the new Jules Verne record, and a destroyer was despatched with the committee and journalists aboard to see us arrive. The waves were making even this substantial vessel roll heavily and with everything liable to erratic surges neither we nor the French destroyer captain wanted the vessels too close to each other. Other boats began to appear, braving the extremely rough seas, and soon we were accompanied by half a dozen whose occupants' stomachs could withstand the motion. In many ways we were having the easiest ride as the boat was very stable and the chains held us steady. From 0800 all the crew were in the cockpit with the exception of myself – who was below navigating – and Jaws – who demonstrated his unswerving sense of priorities by putting the lunch on to soak! Land was sighted at 1032 hours, our first sight of it for seventy-four days, and by now I was in radio contact with David Pelly and John Reed who had come over from England as the official time-keepers for world records. Aware that we were towing so much ironmongery, people did not anticipate a fast finish but in fact we were making 9 knots. I placed the radar bearing mark on Ushant and watched it slowly come round to the south about two miles away. Nearer, nearer, and then we were there. I announced the news to the cockpit and there were yells and cheers whilst I noted down the exact time from the time-keepers – 74 days, 22 hours, 17 minutes and 22 seconds. It looked so bland written down like that, but it was 4 days, 8 hours faster than *Commodore*, a giant leap, and I don't suppose there have been many world sailing records broken so decisively by boats towing anchor chain and warps!

There was no question of taking the route outside Ushant back into Brest, no one in his right mind would have sailed into those waves, so we headed straight for the Canal du Four, recovering the warp as we went. The swell eased inside the islands and we unrolled a little more sail as there was another finish line to pass, the one for the race with *Lyonnaise*. This line passed abeam at 1334 hours and another committee declared us the winner of that race as well. Had it not been for the second line we could have considered sailing straight for Southampton, which was more appropriate as it was our home port, but the weather made this impossible, so we ran on up into the harbour and were towed into the Marina at Moulin Blanc where we had cast off just seventy-five days and a circumnavigation before.

We waited in Brest for *Lyonnaise* who, like us, came in quickly at the end to finish just over two days behind, a sterling effort which made them the fastest French circumnavigators. We leapt on board as they came alongside and I went across to Olivier to congratulate him. He saw me coming.

"I 'ate you!" he grinned, and stretched out his hand.

Records are meant to be challenged and *Enza*'s is unlikely to last beyond 1996. It will take a great deal of luck, though, to beat her time with a boat of similar size. To guarantee a faster run needs, with current technology, a larger craft. In the two years that the Jules Verne Trophy has existed, the world's three largest racing multihulls all completed circumnavigations between 74 days, 22 hours and 79 days, 18 hours, maintaining averages just ahead of 14.5 knots. It is probably a coincidence that the longest boat was fastest and the shortest slowest, but the general rule is that a good big boat will always beat a good little boat, all other factors being equal.

In the first attempt two out of three had to retire through damage caused by exterior objects, a hazard for any future challenge. During the first half of our second voyage the luck was with us all the way, only on the second part did it turn against us and cost perhaps four days. In an event that is dependent upon the unpredictability of weather patterns eight to ten weeks in advance, luck has an important part to play. No one can expect good luck the whole time, but we got it half the time, a reasonable average, and it would be a brave person who would gamble on having more. Although modern ocean-racing monohulls participating in the BOC and Whitbread Races are raising their average speeds the whole time, they are not yet as fast as the multihulls, nor do they race for more than three or four weeks at a time. The fastest time non-stop for one of these craft at the moment is still 109 days. So it is a reasonably safe to bet that when *Enza*'s record is broken it will be by a multihull and one longer than 100 feet. Such a craft could, with luck, break the seventy-day barrier, the next big objective.

APPENDICES

APPENDIX I

Target and Reality

The daily average target for a seventy-seven-day voyage was 354 miles and the average speed required 14.74 knots.

The distances below were calculated from 1300 hours each day.

Latitude	Target Longitude	Day's Run	DAY Start	Latitude	Enza Longitude	Day's Run
48° 28′ N	05° 05′ W	—	**Start**			
43 15 N	09 25 W	360	**1**	43° 09′ N	11° 17′ W	411
38 05 N	13 20 W	360	**2**	37 22 N	15 49 W	404
32 40 N	16 30 W	360	**3**	31 33 N	21 47 W	457
27 40 N	20 00 W	345	**4**	24 05 N	24 09 W	465
22 25 N	22 40 W	345	**5**	16 14 N	26 32 W	490
17 15 N	25 15 W	345	**6**	07 45 N	28 06 W	517
11 25 N	26 50 W	360	**7**	01 04 N	27 09 W	405
06 00 N	26 50 W	330	**8**	04 44 S	30 00 W	388
01 50 N	26 10 W	250	**9**	11 35 S	31 18 W	419
01 10 S	26 10 W	180	**10**	17 55 S	31 27 W	380
04 05 S	26 45 W	180	**11**	24 28 S	30 48 W	395
08 00 S	28 10 W	250	**12**	30 14 S	30 09 W	349
11 55 S	29 35 W	250	**13**	33 28 S	29 23 W	198
16 35 S	31 20 W	300	**14**	35 01 S	28 05 W	112
21 55 S	31 20 W	320	**15**	39 22 S	20 46 W	437
27 15 S	31 20 W	320	**16**	42 19 S	15 30 W	298
32 20 S	29 15 W	320	**17**	42 26 S	07 48 W	342
35 00 S	23 45 W	320	**18**	45 24 S	01 48 E	452
37 40 S	17 40 W	340	**19**	43 44 S	11 08 E	411
38 40 S	10 10 W	360	**20**	43 11 S	21 05 E	435
39 10 S	02 25 W	360	**21**	43 34 S	31 32 E	456
39 40 S	05 20 E	360	**22**	44 53 S	42 31 E	478
40 15 S	13 30 E	380	**23**	43 32 S	51 56 E	413
40 15 S	22 15 E	400	**24**	43 11 S	61 15 E	407
40 15 S	31 15 E	410	**25**	44 20 S	70 52 E	423
40 50 S	40 10 E	410	**26**	44 27 S	81 13 E	443
40 50 S	49 10 E	410	**27**	43 42 E	91 08 E	430

Latitude	Target Longitude	Day's Run	DAY	Latitude	Enza Longitude	Day's Run
48° 28' N	05° 05' W	—	Start			
41 25 S	58 15 E	410	28	44 42 S	100 50 E	422
42 00 S	67 20 E	410	29	42 46 S	109 35 E	370
42 35 S	76 35 E	410	30	44 20 S	117 58 E	376
43 10 S	85 50 E	410	31	44 48 S	128 41 E	459
43 50 S	95 15 E	410	32	47 14 S	139 02 E	456
44 00 S	104 45 E	410	33	48 09 S	149 05 E	409
44 15 S	114 15 E	410	34	53 04 S	155 29 E	383
44 50 S	123 45 E	410	35	58 24 S	162 25 E	398
45 25 S	133 25 E	410	36	59 43 S	175 53 E	424
45 25 S	143 10 E	410	37	61 06 S	170 53 W	399
45 25 S	152 55 E	410	38	61 38 S	157 40 W	381
47 10 S	162 30 E	410	39	61 41 S	148 34 W	259
48 55 S	172 20 E	410	40	61 50 S	145 30 W	88
49 00 S	177 15 W	410	41	60 52 S	133 48 W	341
49 00 S	166 50 W	410	42	61 35 S	120 24 W	390
49 00 S	156 30 W	410	43	62 09 S	103 39 W	475
49 00 S	146 00 W	410	44	61 34 S	92 16 W	324
49 00 S	135 40 W	410	45	60 35 S	88 02 W	136
49 00 S	125 10 W	410	46	60 13 S	79 29 W	254
49 00 S	114 50 W	410	47	58 22 S	75 12 W	172
49 00 S	104 20 W	410	48	57 52 S	68 16 W	221
49 00 S	94 00 W	410	49	55 04 S	59 37 W	332
49 00 S	83 30 W	410	50	53 46 S	50 34 W	326
52 25 S	74 10 W	410	51	51 51 S	42 22 W	319
55 50 S	64 05 W	410	52	47 19 S	32 57 W	456
52 30 S	54 15 W	400	53	40 31 S	27 37 W	469
49 15 S	45 15 W	390	54	35 17 S	25 25 W	331
46 05 S	37 10 W	380	55	33 02 S	25 30 W	135
41 45 S	32 55 W	320	56	30 21 S	24 17 W	173
37 05 S	29 30 W	320	57	25 51 S	23 54 W	270
32 20 S	26 05 W	330	58	20 52 S	24 30 W	302
27 35 S	22 55 W	330	59	14 38 S	25 49 W	381
22 20 S	19 35 W	360	60	08 18 S	26 42 W	383
16 20 S	19 35 W	360	61	02 14 S	27 10 W	364
10 20 S	19 35 W	360	62	00 36 N	28 36 W	191
04 20 S	19 35 W	360	63	03 37 N	31 10 W	239
01 45 S	21 10 W	184	64	08 35 N	34 22 W	353
01 10 N	22 50 W	200	65	13 52 N	37 18 W	361
04 45 N	24 55 W	250	66	20 02 N	39 07 W	384
08 25 N	27 00 W	250	67	25 51 N	39 22 W	350
12 45 N	29 35 W	300	68	30 13 N	39 22 W	262
17 25 N	31 20 W	300	69	34 28 S	38 08 W	265
22 35 N	33 20 W	330	70	36 42 N	38 17 W	135
28 00 N	34 24 W	330	71	40 45 N	33 47 W	321
33 00 N	34 25 W	300	72	41 17 N	26 40 W	324
38 30 N	34 25 W	330	73	44 00 N	18 06 W	412
42 20 N	29 15 W	330	74	47 12 N	10 12 W	380
45 20 N	22 05 W	360	75	48 32 N	05 08 W	220
47 25 N	13 55 W	360	76			
48 28 N	05 05 W	360	77			
		27,239				26,442

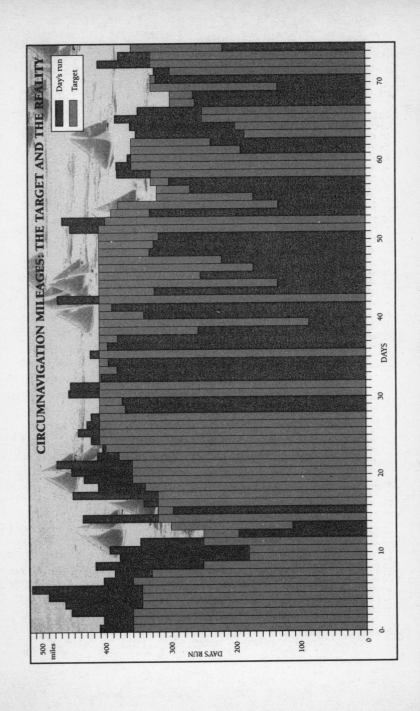

CIRCUMNAVIGATION MILEAGES: THE TARGET AND THE REALITY

APPENDIX II

Times Achieved by *Enza*

Ushant to equator (3,225 miles)	7 days, 4 hours, 24 minutes at an average speed of 18.71 knots
Ushant to Cape of Good Hope	19 days, 17 hours, 53 minutes
Ushant to Cape Leeuwen	29 days, 16 hours, 01 minutes
Ushant to International Date Line	36 days, 9 hours, 49 minutes
Ushant to Cape Horn	48 days, 2 hours, 32 minutes
Ushant to equator (homeward)	61 days, 11 hours, 35 minutes
Ushant to Ushant	**74 days, 22 hours, 17 minutes, 22 seconds**
Equator to equator	54 days, 7 hours, 11 minutes
Cape Horn to equator	13 days, 8 hours, 3 minutes (2 hours, 10 minutes slower than *Commodore*)
Time to crossing outward track on homeward voyage ('tying the knot')	39 days, 5 hours, 51 minutes
Best twenty-four-hour run	520.8 nautical miles
Best ten-day run	4,347.5 miles at an average speed of 18.11 knots
Total distance sailed	26,442.34 miles
Average speed overall	14.70 knots

Enza beat *Commodore*'s time by 4 days, 7 hours, 15 minutes, 35 seconds

APPENDIX III

Bob Rice's Weather Window was so fundamental to the success of our project that I asked him to explain how he became involved in meteorology in the first place and when this led him into weather-routing. I give his explanation in full because it is a fascinating insight into this very technical aspect to ocean voyaging, made even more interesting by the background to the tactics that forced us south off New Zealand at the halfway point, the decision that saved our attempt.

Although the use of specialists based ashore to advise boats how to make the best of the weather conditions is banned from most races, it is allowed in open events like the Jules Verne Trophy.

R.K-J

WEATHER FORECASTING AND WEATHER-ROUTING
by BOB RICE

My career in meteorology spans some forty-one years in total (as this is written), but specialisation in the field of providing met support for adventures, including weather-routing for yachts, really got underway some twenty-three years later. Sure, there were some interesting forecast projects during those earlier times, but the real emergence of the Special Projects type of met support was not really developed until 1978 with the wildly successful transatlantic flight of the *Double Eagle II* balloon in August of that year. As with so many turning points in life, I don't seem to recall that there were any clear indications at the time that both my professional and personal life were suddenly heading off on some entirely new and unexplored tack, and I'm not all that sure what I would have done differently if there had been any indications, even though that tack hasn't all been a broad reach.

Following the *Double Eagle II* flight and its ensuing publicity, I was approached by the American multihull sailor Phil Weld enquiring whether it was possible to develop a similar weather-routing system for his entry in the 1978 Route de Rhum race aboard the trimaran *Rogue Wave*. We discussed this idea at some length and I ultimately wound up providing a full routing system for that race. Communications difficulties diluted the effects somewhat, but it remained a generally successful endeavour, resulting in a close third placing, despite Phil spending some twenty-four hours hove-to in order to repair a halyard.

I've been told by a noted sailing historian that this was the 'birth' of weather-routing for racing sailboats, as opposed to weather forecasts for boats. However, I'd not be so presumptuous as to claim that distinction, since I frankly have no idea as to the history of routing. It was just something that Phil and I decided would work best for him, in order to utilise not only the met expertise, but also to formulate the intense personal relationship that should exist between met support and user in the interests of performance and safety for a special event. After the Route de Rhum, similar procedures were implemented for the 1980 Ostar transatlantic race, resulting in Phil's record-setting win aboard the trimaran *Moxie*. It was fortuitous that both of these initial support programs, balloon and boat, were generated for the type of individual who would give credit and spread the word through the media about their success and the part that our weather had played: Max Anderson of the balloon *Double Eagle II* and Phil Weld from *Moxie*. Both friends. Both gone now.

Over the years this routing service has expanded, in terms of area coverage, and in the details provided for an individual boat, along with an increase in the number of projects.

It was in 1985 that I made my first foray into the vaunted Southern Ocean and became global by providing the weather and routing service for Dodge Morgan on his record 150-day non-stop circumnavigation with *American Promise*. So some seven years of evolution was spun into the learning curve between the first suggested North Atlantic routing service for Phil Weld and the global conquests of Dodge Morgan, and nine more before I came into position to be providing the met support for the catamaran *Enza* some sixteen years after the landing of the *Double Eagle II* in a barley field just short of Paris, France.

But what is weather-routing exactly? After all, everyone comes in contact with weather forecasts, perhaps one of the more ubiquitous commodities known to man. And weather forecasts are weather forecasts, from any source, with all the inherent frailties that that implies, right? Well, sort of. First off, historically, weather forecasts are for a generalised area, encompassing thousands of square miles of sea and/or land and therefore tend to lack significant specific detail. Secondly, even in this day of computer guidance, there still exist many levels of individual competence due to differing performance records of the various models, the individual forecaster's ability to interpret them, the amount of subjective experience-refining input and the timeliness with which the final product is presented. We'll take this one more step and say that in order to make special projects support work, it's necessary for the forecaster to understand the problems of the user, and how to make weather work for the project, as opposed to simply enduring it.

There's no question but that the advent of meteorological forecast models has greatly narrowed the disparity between individual forecasters over the last ten to fifteen years. During my early days as a forecaster the norm was to start literally with a blank sheet of paper and build the forecast by highly subjective methods. That's when forecasting was truly more art than science; and perhaps, not surprisingly, more fun. Further, due to the complexities and speeds with which weather systems evolve, there's never been a human forecaster who could consistently show skill beyond seventy-two hours, and probably forty-eight hours is more realistic. It will be noted that the term forecaster is used in this discussion, not meteorologist. I don't really mean for those terms to be interchangeable in this discussion, since it takes a special insight and imagination to be a good forecaster and not all meteorologists have that ability, nor can it really be taught. We're talking nuts and bolts synoptic meteorologist here, a weather mechanic, as opposed to the more pure scientist.

The models we utilise are currently run out to 240 hours, with varying results as we extend further into time, but in all cases superior to anything that a human can produce, if in fact a human were foolish enough to even attempt a ten-day forecast. I'll guarantee that this particular forecaster isn't even about to try it. Long-range trends maybe; specific prog maps? No way. There are various models available, generally the product of a government weather service, since the costs of developing the models and, in particular, the costs of the super computers required to crunch the extraordinary amounts of data that pour into them every day, are typically beyond the means of commercial forecast offices. There can be vast differences in these models, another indication that we're a long way from perfection, and it is important to be able to evaluate the strength and weakness of each, both in total and on a day-to-day basis. With the aid of computer guidance it's now feasible to carry forecasts out into that previously impossible range of five to ten days, and, more to the point, with some realistic chance that the forecasts will be in the ball park. No one will suggest that these results are anywhere near approaching perfection, or even any reliable consistency, but with some rather remarkable frequency they do offer vital help in signalling a problem ahead, even if the exact specifics are not necessarily accurate.

I dwell on the evolution of the forecast model, since it is important to understand that routing for a racing sailboat would be generally impossible without them, and no matter how talented the individual forecaster may be, if stripped of the model guidance, he would be helpless in honing the advice down into any meaningful long-range tactics. This is not to say that we're blind slaves to these models. Not by a long shot. However, what it does mean is that the models will bring us to a level from which we can then apply subjective input and experience to refine the results into a finished product for the boat in question. This is why the human element can't be replaced in this sequence at this time, and perhaps never will be.

Routing programs that utilise pure computer input in order to create waypoint suggestions are not only insufficient, but potentially quite dangerous. They are based on the assumption that the input forecast model is perfect, and that the boat's performance is precisely as predicted by that boat's polars. A boat's performance in any given wind varies continuously, and significantly, due to boat heel angle, sea states, etc., so that a precise boat heading, based on a wind forecast made to the nearest degree and knot, as is typical with a computer, is absurdly unrealistic. Winds are just not that stable and the variation inherent in any real-time wind is typically 10° and 10 knots or more, even in a very stable pattern, and often with far greater deviations from moment to moment. Further, since the computer assumes a hundred per cent accuracy in building the routing suggestion, it will often lead a boat into a position that is completely wrong for subsequent events, beyond the forecast range, or when that long-range forecast turns out to be totally wrong. There is no room for subjective compromise which, if actually adhered to, will frequently leave a boat hung out to dry in either a non-efficient or potentially dangerous exposure. Weather being what it is, this is a high enough risk anyway, and virtually guaranteed with blind computer adherence.

A routing service takes a weather forecast and breaks it down for specific projected boat positions and it is accompanied by specific waypoint suggestions in an attempt to enhance the boat's performance or minimise its weakness in working toward a destination goal. This requires total co-operation and understanding between boat and router, both in preliminary concept and in real-time execution. I don't feel that it's my job, the router's job, to dictate a specific waypoint, implying that there are bottomless pits existing on either side of that point. Rather, I would feel that it's my function to define a corridor that's acceptable, so that the skipper can have the flexibility of selecting the best heading angles for performance and downwind considerations, but within certain limitations. I view it all as a bowling alley, in which the boat has the whole alley in which to seek best performance, but only after defining the gutters that it should not wander off into. This can be defined as a slot or, in some cases, it will be defined as a point or boundary which the boat shouldn't pass, due to some form of wasteland on the other side. To this end, we are constantly looking out through that eight- to ten-day period, trying to keep the boat in the best possible position relative to developing roadblocks ahead. This will not eliminate adverse weather, but we would hope to minimise it and to prepare the crew for it when it's unavoidable. And, the longer the voyage, the greater the odds are that significant weather will be a factor at various points along the route.

Since weather features typically move faster than even the fastest sailboats, about all we can do is attempt to position the boat so as best to encounter these systems. The accomplishment of that task can still leave the whole boat vulnerable to something else downstream, but as with most things in life, the compromise required will sometimes trade one evil for another one; but hopefully a lesser one. However, it is also important to remember that looking out even ten days is stretching the capability considerably, so avoiding the problems of today does not mean that there aren't more to come up for the future.

To illustrate the above problem, it's not necessary to go any further than taking a look at the decision-making process for one of the more critical deviations by the catamaran *Enza*, the decision to dive southward around the longitude of Tasmania. The pre-departure plan was to remain at fairly low latitude for the passage south of New Zealand and on into the South Pacific, using the big cat's maximum advantage, to be found in the typical reaching conditions of the lower latitudes, say around the 40°S–54°S latitude band. However, our long-range projection suggested the risk of a slow-moving, or blocked, gale developing around the South Island of New Zealand, which was projected to, and did, bring gale easterlies down past 50°S, which then lasted for some time. The problem with bringing gale easterlies southward like that is not only the obvious, the introduction of long-duration gale easterlies pretty much where we wanted to go, but that it also brings down, by definition, a col. A col is that area between two like pressure-pattern circulations in which there is little or no wind at all. In this case, consider a col as a buffer zone that separates the easterlies of the gale from the prevailing westerlies to the south. On Monday, 14th February, while the boat was pretty much on the desired latitude of 43°S, I advised *Enza* of this impending problem for the following Sunday/ Monday period, and that we should now route with the goal of having the 'flexibility of getting south quickly if necessary', guarding against this possibility as suggested on the seven-day forecast. On Tuesday, 15th February this suggestion was amplified and the suggested reactions escalated. The statement was that "Current long range still suggesting significant complications around NZ for weekend and think it's time we start to guard against results." Then, later in the same message: "Will place confidence on this sequence as being high enough to start leaning toward protection, but not high enough to pull all eggs in that basket. However, would think no other reason inhibits coming on down, so setting up for this possibility should not jeopardise anything else. As such, will suggest your current headings toward 50°S/150°E just about right, and we'll let it go at that for moment, re-evaluating as we go along, with idea that it might be desired to keep on toward 55°S or higher." Still later in the same (lengthy) message: "Don't really want to see you enter Pacific that high, but we'll have to take what's given. In meantime, 50°S looks like good staging area." For Wednesday, 16th February, with the boat now near 44°41′S/127°33′E, the statement read: "By 12Z/Sat we will still indicate potential rat's nest developing ahead . . . everything continues to suggest necessity to be down around 55°S by late Sun/Mon (GMT) period." And then, ". . . suggest no urgency, but southing required for later factors. Best headings for boat and speed . . . suggest headings generally for waypoints around 50°S/150°E and then 55°S/175°E. Those should give us room to play if NZ scenario is still a factor." For Thursday, 17th February, with boat now at 46°41′S/136°56′E, the following was transmitted: "First things first, and that's continuing suggestion that 55°S, at least, will be desired by 12Z/Sun. That's about 24 hours earlier than yesterday's comments, and/or a waypoint now of 55°/165°E. The intermediate of 50°S/150°E still looks OK, but only as a generality. It's the 55°S waypoint that's looking fairly significant by either 165°E and/or 12Z/Sun. Vulnerable area now looking to be from 165°E to 175°W and could require 57°S to 58°S. But, think headings and waypoints as we're using now adequate to be able to move either way as required." Then, the added comment that falls nicely into the famous last words category: "Long range at the moment indicates no problem coming back into lower latitudes after this episode."

As it turned out, this was never really possible, without losing a great deal of east distance and/or time, but does serve to illustrate that we had every intention of coming back north to the lower latitudes once free of this gale and col to the south of New Zealand. By Friday,

18th February, the gale was about ready to trigger near Canterbury Bight for the 12Z/Sat period, which prompted the statement, "For now will suggest, with certain sense of urgency, waypoints of 51°S/ 155°E, 57°S/165°E, 59°S/175°E, 53°S/165°W." The boat was near 47°38'S/147°20'E at the time. By Saturday, 19th February the gale and col were in position, which prompted the message: "Will suggest you remain on starboard and ride it down as far as 59°S. Ice aside, from a met standpoint, feel best to continue the 59°S waypoint to 165°E. Basic suggestion is to get down past 58°S within next 24–30 hours, then take favoured tack for casting between 58°S and 60°S for the Sun/Mon/Tue period." With the boat at 59°56'S/171°56'E for Monday, 21st February the early statement would read: "Would think no more than about 5–10 knots [of breeze] now at 58°S. Would guess you're about directly south of col now, maybe at about 56°S/175°E. Light and variables continue to press southward and think your current position becomes a parking lot within 12–24 hours, and stays that way on into Wednesday . . . vital you not stray too far north from 60°S, maybe 59°30'S as extreme limit for next 24–36 hours." Then, as somewhat of an afterthought: "Things remain edgy though, as bubble high develops around 63°S/175°W, in old ridge, for 12Z/Wed and chases you while coming up to east-north-east."

So, this was the sequence of events that led to the dive southward to, and past, 60°S. As noted, this action was made necessary by the gale centre, since the col was an effect, not a cause. So in a sense, part of the dive was to avoid the gale easterlies, but then we had to keep going to also avoid the light variables in the buffer col. As it turned out, that bubble high, noted rather casually, did, in fact, overrun the boat, the result being a twenty-four-hour average of about 2 knots for the period from 1030Z Thursday, 24th February through 0815Z Friday, 25th February, including a lengthy night-time high pressure becalming – at 62°S latitude. That one episode, the small bubble high pressure centre of perhaps a couple hundred miles in diameter, was timed and placed just exactly wrong to set the table for the subsequent inability to come back north. This prohibited the boat from getting into the proper relationship with the migratory features, as she stalled out in the slow-moving little high. The winds turned to north-west as she shook loose from the high on 26th February, at about 61°21'S/

137°00'W, and for all practical purposes it remained a beat the rest of the way to the Horn.

So, in this one incident we have the highs and lows, so to speak, of weather-routing. Coming south was an absolute necessity, with the option having been to lose as many as five or six days to light and variable and/or easterly directions, and that strategy worked perfectly. However, the next phase was to have been to come northward to a more logical latitude, after having bypassed that particular crisis. With the light high then taking dead aim on the boat, nicely fuelling the forecaster's natural paranoia tendencies in the process, the down-stream strategy was pretty well eliminated and it became a matter of toughing it out in the north gradients and among the icebergs. As it turned out, the patterns across the lower latitudes weren't necessarily a bed of roses either, as the Whitbread boats were discovering, but being north would have eliminated the ice problem and provided somewhat better wind angles.

While the position of the boat at those latitudes was considerably less than desirable, it was preferable to the unacceptable loss of time that would have ensued otherwise. Of course, it's easy enough to state that now, since there weren't any disastrous results from the ice encounters or the high wind/high seas periods while on the wind – and the record was accomplished. However, there is, of course, no argument about the real-time discomfort for the crew by being in that position, nor the risks involved, but then, that's how records are set. There were a couple of times in which coming north would have been possible, but neither of those excursions could have been accomplished without losing both distance and time by several days of north-westerly headings, and these were summarily rejected by the crew. As such, I would view those routing decisions across the South Pacific as being correct.

The decisions in the South Atlantic, both south and northbound, were a good deal more subtle and revolved mainly around trying to sneak around the usual array of subtropical high pressure. These routing suggestions were made based on real-time forecast projections, but also with climatology as a significant input. All things considered it's perhaps true that the routing through the South Atlantic is the most important of an entire circumnavigation, and

I'd also suspect that, if this record is to be broken, most of that time will be saved in the South Atlantic. Not by any breakthrough in routing philosophy, but by carefully playing a favourable pattern, since at any given time the South Atlantic is the area in which one is more apt to find the way strewn with land mines, due to the variability of features, but most of which revolve around flat subtropical high pressure. Multihulls shouldn't be as intimidated by the inter-tropical convergence zone (ITCZ) or doldrums and, *Enza*'s dive into the South Pacific notwithstanding, the routing through the Southern Oceans doesn't lend itself to breakthroughs, so I feel that it's quite likely that it will be the South Atlantic that will tend to make or break another record attempt. It's my admittedly biased opinion that that will only be accomplished with the help of a router.

Bob Rice
25th October 1994